"This series is a tremendous resource for thos
understanding of how the gospel is woven t
pastors and scholars doing gospel business frc
logical feast preparing God's people to apply the entire Bible to all of life with heart and mind
wholly committed to Christ's priorities."

BRYAN CHAPELL, President Emeritus, Covenant Theological Seminary; Senior Pastor,
Grace Presbyterian Church, Peoria, Illinois

"Mark Twain may have smiled when he wrote to a friend, 'I didn't have time to write you a
short letter, so I wrote you a long letter.' But the truth of Twain's remark remains serious and
universal, because well-reasoned, compact writing requires extra time and extra hard work.
And this is what we have in the Crossway Bible study series *Knowing the Bible*. The skilled au-
thors and notable editors provide the contours of each book of the Bible as well as the grand
theological themes that bind them together as one Book. Here, in a 12-week format, are care-
fully wrought studies that will ignite the mind and the heart."

R. KENT HUGHES, Visiting Professor of Practical Theology, Westminster Theological
Seminary

"*Knowing the Bible* brings together a gifted team of Bible teachers to produce a high-quality
series of study guides. The coordinated focus of these materials is unique: biblical content,
provocative questions, systematic theology, practical application, and the gospel story of God's
grace presented all the way through Scripture."

PHILIP G. RYKEN, President, Wheaton College

"These *Knowing the Bible* volumes provide a significant and very welcome variation on the
general run of inductive Bible studies. This series provides substantial instruction, as well as
teaching through the very questions that are asked. *Knowing the Bible* then goes even further
by showing how any given text links with the gospel, the whole Bible, and the formation of
theology. I heartily endorse this orientation of individual books to the whole Bible and the
gospel, and I applaud the demonstration that sound theology was not something invented
later by Christians, but is right there in the pages of Scripture."

GRAEME L. GOLDSWORTHY, former lecturer, Moore Theological College; author,
According to Plan, Gospel and Kingdom, The Gospel in Revelation, and *Gospel and Wisdom*

"What a gift to earnest, Bible-loving, Bible-searching believers! The organization and structure
of the Bible study format presented through the *Knowing the Bible* series is so well conceived.
Students of the Word are led to understand the content of passages through perceptive, guided
questions, and they are given rich insights and application all along the way in the brief but
illuminating sections that conclude each study. What potential growth in depth and breadth
of understanding these studies offer! One can only pray that vast numbers of believers will
discover more of God and the beauty of his Word through these rich studies."

BRUCE A. WARE, Professor of Christian Theology, The Southern Baptist Theological
Seminary

KNOWING THE BIBLE

J. I. Packer, Theological Editor
Dane C. Ortlund, Series Editor
Lane T. Dennis, Executive Editor

•   •   •   •   •   •

Genesis	Psalms	Jonah, Micah, and Nahum	Ephesians
Exodus	Proverbs		Philippians
Leviticus	Ecclesiastes	Haggai, Zechariah, and Malachi	Colossians and Philemon
Numbers	Song of Solomon		
Deuteronomy	Isaiah	Matthew	1–2 Thessalonians
Joshua	Jeremiah	Mark	1–2 Timothy and Titus
Judges	Lamentations, Habakkuk, and Zephaniah	Luke	
Ruth and Esther		John	
1–2 Samuel		Acts	Hebrews
1–2 Kings	Ezekiel	Romans	James
1–2 Chronicles	Daniel	1 Corinthians	1–2 Peter and Jude
Ezra and Nehemiah	Hosea	2 Corinthians	1–3 John
Job	Joel, Amos, and Obadiah	Galatians	Revelation

•   •   •   •   •   •

J. I. PACKER was the former Board of Governors' Professor of Theology at Regent College (Vancouver, BC). Dr. Packer earned his DPhil at the University of Oxford. He is known and loved worldwide as the author of the best-selling book *Knowing God*, as well as many other titles on theology and the Christian life. He served as the General Editor of the ESV Bible and as the Theological Editor for the *ESV Study Bible*.

LANE T. DENNIS is CEO of Crossway, a not-for-profit publishing ministry. Dr. Dennis earned his PhD from Northwestern University. He is Chair of the ESV Bible Translation Oversight Committee and Executive Editor of the *ESV Study Bible*.

DANE C. ORTLUND (PhD, Wheaton College) serves as senior pastor of Naperville Presbyterian Church in Naperville, Illinois. He is an editor for the Knowing the Bible series and the Short Studies in Biblical Theology series, and is the author of several books, including *Gentle and Lowly: The Heart of Christ for Sinners and Sufferers*.

1–2 TIMOTHY AND TITUS

A 12-WEEK STUDY

Brian J. Tabb

:: CROSSWAY®

WHEATON, ILLINOIS

Crossway is a publishing ministry of Good News Publishers.

VP		31	30	29	28	27	26	25	24	23
15	14	13	12	11	10	9	8	7	6	5

TABLE OF CONTENTS

SERIES PREFACE

KNOWING THE BIBLE, as the series title indicates, was created to help readers know and understand the meaning, the message, and the God of the Bible. Each volume in the series consists of 12 units that progressively take the reader through a clear, concise study of that book of the Bible. In this way, any given volume can fruitfully be used in a 12-week format either in group study, such as in a church-based context, or in individual study. Of course, these 12 studies could be completed in fewer or more than 12 weeks, as convenient, depending on the context in which they are used.

Each study unit gives an overview of the text at hand before digging into it with a series of questions for reflection or discussion. The unit then concludes by highlighting the gospel of grace in each passage ("Gospel Glimpses"), identifying whole-Bible themes that occur in the passage ("Whole-Bible Connections"), and pinpointing Christian doctrines that are affirmed in the passage ("Theological Soundings").

The final component to each unit is a section for reflecting on personal and practical implications from the passage at hand. The layout provides space for recording responses to the questions proposed, and we think readers need to do this to get the full benefit of the exercise. The series also includes definitions of key words. These definitions are indicated by a note number in the text and are found at the end of each chapter.

Lastly, to help understand the Bible in this deeper way, we urge readers to use the ESV Bible and the *ESV Study Bible*, which are available in various print and digital formats, including online editions at esv.org. The Knowing the Bible series is also available online.

May the Lord greatly bless your study as you seek to know him through knowing his Word.

J. I. Packer
Lane T. Dennis

WEEK 1: OVERVIEW

⏶

First and Second Timothy and Titus are among Paul's most personal and practical letters. Paul writes to his spiritual children Timothy and Titus in order to instruct and encourage them in gospel ministry. These books are often called the Pastoral Epistles because they focus significantly on the character and responsibilities of those who teach and lead God's church. However, these letters apply broadly to all Christians and include some of the most explicit biblical teaching on various topics, including:

- the difference between true and false teaching (1 Tim. 1:3–11);
- the power of the gospel to save sinners (1 Tim. 1:12–16);
- the goodness of God's creation (1 Tim. 4:4);
- the dangers of pride and the love of money (1 Tim. 6:4–10);
- the divine quality and effectiveness of the Scriptures (2 Tim. 3:15–17); and,
- the vital importance of good works in the Christian life (Titus 2:14; 3:14).

Above all, Paul stresses that the gospel of Jesus Christ saves and transforms sinners, and this gospel is the "good deposit" that should be protected and passed on to others through intentional discipleship (1 Tim. 6:20; 2 Tim. 1:14; 2:1–2).

First Timothy stresses the need to confront false teaching in Ephesus and to promote a positive vision for doctrine, order, and conduct in God's household, the church. Timothy must guard the gospel and also set an example to the believers in his speech, conduct, love, faith, and purity (4:12; 6:20).

Second Timothy is Paul's farewell discourse to his "beloved child" (1:2). Although Paul is in chains for Christ, he rejoices that God's Word is "not bound," and he eagerly anticipates final salvation and glory (2:8–10). Paul charges Timothy to preach the Word, endure suffering, and entrust the apostolic gospel to faithful men who will teach others (2:2–3; 4:2).

Titus stresses that the gospel and good works are inseparable. Paul directs his coworker to appoint qualified elders in Crete (1:5–9), rebuke false teachers (1:10–16), and model sound doctrine and good works (2:1; 3:14).

Placing These Letters in the Larger Story

God created his world, and it was very good. Then sin brought disorder, devastation, and death for God's world and humanity. The Old Testament portrays God's patience with his rebellious covenant people and his promises to rescue sinners and restore his broken world. The New Testament announces that God has fulfilled his ancient promises and demonstrated his goodness and loving kindness by sending Jesus Christ, our Savior. The Gospels narrate the life, death, and resurrection of the Savior and King Jesus Christ. Acts records how Jesus' followers continued his mission by proclaiming the gospel in the power of the Holy Spirit among all nations. The Epistles provide apostolic instruction for believers living between Jesus' first and second comings.

Paul's letters to Timothy and Titus beautifully summarize the gospel message: "Christ Jesus came into the world to save sinners" (1 Tim. 1:15); he "gave himself for us to redeem us from all lawlessness and to purify for himself a people for his own possession who are zealous for good works" (Titus 2:14). This glorious good news is the standard for sound doctrine and the motivation for godliness. These three letters promote sound teaching and godly leadership in the church while warning against false teaching and ungodly leadership.

Key Verses

"I hope to come to you soon, but I am writing these things to you so that, if I delay, you may know how one ought to behave in the household of God, which is the church of the living God, a pillar and buttress of the truth" (1 Tim. 3:14–15).

"You then, my child, be strengthened by the grace that is in Christ Jesus, and what you have heard from me in the presence of many witnesses entrust to faithful men, who will be able to teach others also" (2 Tim. 2:1–2).

"The saying is trustworthy, and I want you to insist on these things, so that those who have believed in God may be careful to devote themselves to good works. These things are excellent and profitable for people" (Titus 3:8).

Date and Historical Background

Paul wrote 1 Timothy and Titus in order to encourage and instruct his coworkers in difficult ministry situations in Ephesus and Crete. Timothy and Titus were to confront false teaching and promote order and godly conduct in the church. Some interpreters argue that Paul wrote these two letters in the mid-50s, identifying Paul's journey to Macedonia in 1 Timothy 1:3 with Acts 20:1, where Paul travels to Macedonia after the riot in Ephesus. Others date these letters to the mid-60s, following Paul's first imprisonment in Rome (Acts 28:16).

Paul wrote 2 Timothy near the end of his life, during his second imprisonment in Rome, in the mid- to late-60s. Paul had "fought the good fight" and "kept the faith" (2 Tim. 4:7), and he charged Timothy not to be ashamed of the gospel but to follow his example of faithful ministry in suffering (1:8, 13). Paul also asked Timothy to visit him soon in prison (4:9).

Outline of 1 Timothy

I. Doctrine Makes a Difference (1:1–20)

   A. Paul's greeting to Timothy (1:1–2)

   B. Timothy's charge to confront false teaching (1:3–11)

   C. Paul's gratitude for gospel grace (1:12–17)

   D. Timothy's charge restated (1:18–20)

II. Gospel-Shaped Living and Leadership in God's Household (2:1–3:16)

   A. Gospel-shaped prayer and orderly worship (2:1–15)

   B. Gospel-shaped leadership (3:1–13)

   C. The mystery of godliness (3:14–16)

III. Instructions for the Church and Its Leaders (4:1–6:2a)

   A. False teaching in later times (4:1–5)

   B. Teach and model sound doctrine (4:6–16)

   C. Encourage older and younger believers (5:1–2)

   D. Honor widows (5:3–16)

    E. Honor elders (5:17–25)

    F. Honor masters (6:1–2a)

IV. Contrast between True and False Teaching (6:2b–21)

    A. Negative: False teachers motivated by gain (6:2b–10)

    B. Positive: Godly teachers motivated by eternal life (6:11–16)

    C. Charge to the wealthy (6:17–19)

    D. Guard the gospel (6:20–21)

▶ Outline of 2 Timothy

V. Suffering for Christ (1:1–2:7)

    A. Paul's greeting to Timothy (1:1–2)

    B. Paul's gratitude for Timothy's sincere faith (1:3–5)

    C. Suffer for the gospel by God's power (1:6–11)

    D. Examples of fearless faithfulness (1:12–18)

    E. Entrust the gospel to faithful men (2:1–7)

VI. Dealing with Opposition in the Church (2:8–3:9)

    A. Remember Jesus Christ and the promises of the gospel (2:8–13)

    B. Faithful ministers rightly handle the Word (2:14–21)

    C. Faithful ministers pursue righteousness and avoid quarrels (2:22–26)

    D. Difficulty in the last days (3:1–9)

VII. The Minister's Conduct, Commitment, and Charge (3:10–4:8)

    A. Hold fast to Scripture and Paul's example (3:10–17)

    B. Preach the Word (4:1–8)

VIII. Concluding Instructions (4:9–22)

▶ Outline of Titus

IX. Appoint Elders (1:1–16)

    A. Paul's greeting to Titus (1:1–4)

    B. Titus's charge: Establish order, appoint elders (1:5–9)

    C. Titus's challenge: False teachers (1:10–16)

X. Teach Sound Doctrine (2:1–15)

    A. Good works for God's people (2:1–10)

    B. The gospel foundation for good works (2:11–15)

XI. Saved for Good (3:1–15)

    A. Good works toward outsiders (3:1–2)

    B. The gospel foundation for good works (3:3–8)

    C. Avoid controversies and division (3:9–11)

    D. Concluding instructions (3:12–15)

As You Get Started

As you begin this study, do you have a sense of specific emphases in Paul's letters to Timothy and Titus? Without consulting your Bible, are there any particular passages that come to mind? Have these letters been meaningful for your own walk with the Lord in any specific ways?

What is your current understanding of what 1–2 Timothy and Titus contribute to Christian theology? That is, how do these letters clarify our understanding of God, Jesus Christ, sin, salvation, the end times, or other doctrines?

What aspects of these three epistles have confused you? Are there any specific questions you hope to have answered through this study?

As You Finish This Unit . . .

Take a few minutes to ask God to bless you with increased understanding and a transformed heart and life as you begin this study of Paul's letters to Timothy and Titus.

WEEK 2: DOCTRINE MAKES A DIFFERENCE

1 Timothy 1:1–20

The Place of the Passage

Paul writes to his dear coworker Timothy with apostolic authority and urgency. Most of Paul's other letters begin with a greeting, followed by a lengthy thanksgiving and prayer. But in 1 Timothy and Titus, Paul moves immediately from a greeting to his reason for writing. Paul urges Timothy to remain at Ephesus to confront false teachers, who lack love, sincere faith, and understanding of the law and sound doctrine (1 Tim. 1:3–11). Paul thanks God for showing mercy to himself, the "foremost" sinner (1:12–17). Paul's testimony of personal transformation illustrates the truth and power of the gospel, which contrasts with the impotence of the false teaching circulating in Ephesus. Paul then restates his charge to Timothy (1:18–20).

The Big Picture

In 1 Timothy 1, Paul charges Timothy to confront false teachers and to hold fast to the gospel that glorifies God and saves sinners.

> ## Reflection and Discussion

Read through the complete passage for this study, 1 Timothy 1:1–20. Then review the questions below concerning this introductory section to 1 Timothy and write your notes on them. (For further background, see the *ESV Study Bible*, pages 2325–2327; available online at esv.org.)

1. Paul's Greeting to Timothy (1:1–2)

Paul introduces himself as "an apostle of Christ Jesus" (1 Tim. 1:1; compare 2 Tim. 1:1; Titus 1:1). This title signals Paul's status as an authoritative leader called by the Messiah Jesus and commissioned as his ambassador. Why do you think he stresses his apostleship in this letter to his close friend Timothy? How does Paul's apostolic authority relate to his reason for writing 1 Timothy? Compare 1:3; 3:14–15.

Paul addresses this urgent apostolic letter to "Timothy, my true child in the faith" (1 Tim. 1:2). Similarly, he calls Timothy "my beloved child" in 2 Timothy 1:2 (see also 1 Tim. 1:18; 2 Tim. 2:1; 1 Cor. 4:17; Phil. 2:22). Why does Paul describe Timothy in this way? How might Paul's opening words encourage Timothy in his challenging mission (1 Tim. 1:3)? How should the Ephesian church respond to Timothy as the apostle Paul's "true child"?

Paul begins all of his letters with the prayer "grace and peace" (1 Tim. 1:2). Grace (*charis*) adapts the Greek salutation "greetings" (*chairein*) and stresses God's un-deserved favor through Jesus Christ (1 Tim. 1:14; Titus 2:11). Likewise, "peace" adapts the Jewish greeting *shalom*, which denotes wholeness and blessing. Jesus secures our peace with God (Rom. 5:1) and with one another (Eph. 2:14). First Timothy 1:2 and 2 Timothy 1:2 also include the word "mercy," which occurs only in these two greetings. What stands out to you about God's mercy in 1 Timothy 1:13, 16, and 2 Timothy 1:2, 16, 18? Why do you think Paul prays for Timothy to experience God's mercy?

2. Timothy's Charge to Confront False Teaching (1:3–11)

According to 1 Timothy 1:3–7, what is the problem with the content and fruits of the "different doctrine" some were teaching in Ephesus?

How does Paul contrast (in 1 Tim. 1:3–7) his aim and motivation with that of the false teachers? Note at least three differences.

The false teachers seek to teach the law but lack true understanding of it (1 Tim. 1:7). Paul and his coworkers, on the other hand, understand the law's goodness and proper use (1:8). The "law" refers to the law given to Moses, and the verses that follow include several significant parallels with Exodus 20:2–17. List allusions to the Ten Commandments found in 1 Timothy 1:9–10.

Christians have often taught that there are three primary uses of the law: (1) to reveal sin, (2) to restrain wrongdoers from committing more grievous sin, and (3) to instruct believers concerning God's will for our lives. Which of these uses of the law does Paul emphasize in 1 Timothy 1:8–10?

---

3. Paul's Gratitude for Gospel Grace (1:12–17)

Why does Paul thank Jesus in 1 Timothy 1:12–14? How do these verses relate to the occasion of the letter, described in 1:3–7? In what ways did Paul's previous life apart from Christ resemble the false teachers Timothy must confront? Compare 1 Timothy 1:6–7, 20; 6:3–4.

Why did Paul receive mercy, according to 1 Timothy 1:12–13? How does Paul's appointment as an apostle showcase the lavish grace and perfect patience of Jesus Christ (1:16)? How might you explain to someone else your own experience of Christ's saving mercy?

First Timothy 1:15 is the first of several "trustworthy sayings" found in Paul's letters to Timothy and Titus. Look up 1 Timothy 3:1; 4:9; 2 Timothy 2:11; and

Titus 3:8. What do these "sayings" emphasize about the gospel and godly leadership in the church? How should we respond to these truths?

4. Timothy's Charge Restated (1:18–20)

Paul reminds Timothy of the "prophecies previously made about you," which probably refers to Timothy's calling and equipping for ministry (1:18; compare 4:14). How might these prophecies help Timothy to fulfill his charge?

Paul "handed over" his opponents Hymenaeus and Alexander to Satan (1 Tim. 1:20). First Corinthians 5:5 describes the final step of church discipline in similar terms. Church discipline is not vindictive or mean-spirited; it aims to protect and purify the church and to restore the sinner. Why was this action necessary to protect the church at Ephesus (see 2 Tim. 2:16–18)?

Read through the following three sections on *Gospel Glimpses*, *Whole-Bible Connections*, and *Theological Soundings*. Then take time to consider the *Personal Implications* these sections may have for you.

Gospel Glimpses

TRUTH AND LOVE. Truth and love belong together. Faithful ministers must guard the gospel and confront false teaching that distracts and damages the church. Right doctrine is essential, but it is a means to an end. The church must preserve the truth for the sake of grace-saturated, faith-driven, Christ-exalting *love* (1 Tim. 1:5). Such love fulfills the law (Rom. 13:8–10) and flows from being united to Jesus Christ (1 Tim. 1:14). Sound doctrine without love misses the very essence of true Christianity (John 13:35; Rev. 2:2–4). Love cannot flourish or endure in times of trial apart from the nourishment and motivation of sound doctrine. The gospel is the standard of truth and the catalyst for love.

EXTRAVAGANT MERCY. Paul remembers that he was a blasphemer, persecutor, insolent opponent, and chief of sinners. He was an ignorant, unbelieving rebel, like the false teachers at Ephesus. Then, while Paul was traveling to persecute the church in Damascus, the Lord Jesus appeared to him and showered him with mercy and grace (Acts 9:1–16; 1 Tim. 1:15). This is one of the clearest summaries of the gospel anywhere in Scripture, and Paul stresses that it is "trustworthy and deserving of full acceptance." God's mercy can reach anyone, even a zealous persecutor like Paul. This precious truth transformed Paul's identity and ministry, and it should do the same for us.

Whole-Bible Connections

THE LAW IS GOOD. The law is "good" (1 Tim. 1:8; compare Rom. 7:12, 16). God graciously revealed his law to Israel after rescuing them from slavery in Egypt (Ex. 20:2) and calling them to be his special people by reflecting his holiness (Ex. 19:5–6; Lev. 11:45). The law established the terms of God's covenant with Israel. Those who obey would be blessed, while rebels would be cursed (Leviticus 26). Jesus Christ fulfilled that law (Matt. 5:17; Rom. 10:4): he perfectly embodied the grace and truth to which the law pointed (John 1:17), and he bore the curse of the law that we deserved (Gal. 3:13). First Timothy 1:8–9 clarifies that the law must be used "lawfully," according to its intent. Its purpose of restraining sin is not for "the just" (those who do what is right) but for "the lawless and disobedient," to keep them from further wickedness. Christians are "not under the law" in this sense (Gal. 5:18). The gospel, not the law, is the foundation for Christian doctrine and practice (1 Tim. 1:11).

Theological Soundings

GLORY. Human beings are made to delight in glory and transcendent greatness. We celebrate gold medalists and give standing ovations after brilliant performances. These responses to human glory are pointers to our ultimate design: God made us to see and savor his resplendent glory forever. The glory of God is the summation of the beauty and perfection of God himself. In 1 Timothy 1:11, Paul refers to "the gospel of the *glory* of the blessed God." That is, the gospel displays God's impeccable character and matchless worth. In 1:16–17, Paul reflects on his personal experience of God's saving mercy in Christ and responds fittingly with worship. God's glory will one day illuminate the whole new creation (Rev. 21:23), and his redeemed people will experience consummate delight in seeing and celebrating his supreme glory forever.

A GOOD CONSCIENCE. "Conscience" is a person's sense of what he or she believes to be right or wrong. Paul's charge to Timothy is motivated by a "good conscience" (1 Tim. 1:5), and Timothy must maintain "faith and a good conscience" in his ministry (1:19; compare 3:9). A *good* conscience accurately reflects God's revealed standards for right and wrong and guides a person's judgments and actions. When our hearts are pure and we think and behave consistently with a good conscience, the fruit is love (1:5). Someone with a *seared* conscience has lost all bearings for what is right or wrong, true or false (4:2); that person feels no remorse or guilt for sinning against God or promoting false teaching. The conscience is a gift from God that we should consistently heed and keep tuned to God's standards of truth.

▶ Personal Implications

Take time to reflect on the implications of 1 Timothy 1:1–20 for your own life today. Consider what you have learned that might lead you to praise God, repent of sin, and trust in his gracious promises. Make notes below on the personal implications for your walk with the Lord of the (1) *Gospel Glimpses*, (2) *Whole-Bible Connections*, (3) *Theological Soundings*, and (4) this passage as a whole.

1. Gospel Glimpses

2. Whole-Bible Connections

3. Theological Soundings

4. 1 Timothy 1:1–20

As You Finish This Unit . . .

Take a moment now to ask for the Lord's blessing and help as you continue in this study of 1–2 Timothy and Titus. And take a moment also to look back through this unit of study to reflect on some key things that the Lord may be teaching you.

Week 3: Gospel-Shaped Living and Leadership in God's Household

1 Timothy 2:1–3:16

First Timothy 2–3 stresses how the gospel message should impact Christian living and leadership. The gospel of grace has indelibly marked Paul's own life (1:12–17), and Paul now explains how this gospel should shape believers' prayers, priorities, and relationships (2:1–15). He then presents a vision for a church leadership comprised of godly overseers and deacons (3:1–13).

First Timothy's key verses are 3:14–16. Paul writes Timothy this letter so that "you may know how one ought to behave in the household of God." The church proclaims and protects the truth, "the mystery of godliness." This mystery is God's hidden plan that has been made known through Jesus' incarnation, death, resurrection, and exaltation. The church believes and proclaims this glorious gospel truth and shows its transformational power through godly living.

The Big Picture

In 1 Timothy 2:1–3:16, Paul explains how the gospel of Jesus Christ transforms the lives of men, women, overseers, and deacons in God's household, the church.

> ### Reflection and Discussion

Read through the complete passage for this study, 1 Timothy 2:1–3:16. Then review the questions below concerning this section of 1 Timothy and write your notes on them. (For further background, see the *ESV Study Bible*, pages 2327–2331; available online at esv.org.)

1. Gospel-Shaped Prayer and Orderly Worship (2:1–15)

First Timothy 2 presents a positive vision for how men and women should "behave in the household of God" (3:15). First, Paul urges believers to pray. The four terms in 2:1—"supplications, prayers, intercessions, and thanksgivings"—stress a comprehensive life of prayer. What specifically should believers pray for (vv. 1–2)? How should the truths in verses 3–6 shape and motivate prayer?

List the references to "all" and "all people" in verses 1–6. How might the references to "all" and Paul's self-description as a "teacher of the Gentiles" (2:7) contrast with the beliefs and practices of the false teachers at Ephesus, who emphasized the Jewish law, myths, and genealogies (1:4, 7)? How does Paul's focus on "all" stir your heart for prayer and gospel witness across cultural or social boundaries?

In 2:8–15, Paul stresses that God's people should pursue unity, order, and good works when they gather for worship. What practices and attitudes should

Christian men pursue or avoid (v. 8)? How does this relate to the qualifications for overseers (3:1–7)?

What actions should Christian women pursue or avoid (2:9–12)? Why does this matter? Compare this list to the description of godly widows in 5:9–10.

What reasons does Paul give for not permitting a woman to teach or exercise authority over a man in the church (2:12–14)? If possible, consult the commentary on these verses in the *ESV Study Bible*, page 2328, and respond below to what you read.

2. Gospel-Shaped Leadership (3:1–13)

First Timothy 3:1–7 presents a profile of a qualified overseer for the church. In 1 Timothy 5:17, Paul refers to "elders who rule well." What is the relationship between the terms "overseer" and "elder"? Consider Titus 1:5–9; Acts 20:17, 28; 1 Peter 5:1–2.

Overseers and deacons must be "the husband of one wife" or "a man of one woman" (1 Tim. 3:2, 12; Titus 1:6). This qualification may mean (1) leaders must be married; (2) they must marry only once, prohibiting remarriage after a spouse's death or divorce; (3) they must not marry multiple women, prohibiting polygamy; or (4) they must remain faithful to their wives. Which of these interpretations best fits the context of 1 Timothy 3?

What does Paul mean by the qualification "able to teach" (3:2), and why is this essential to the duties of an overseer or elder? Consider 1 Timothy 5:17; 2 Timothy 2:24–25; Titus 1:9.

Paul stresses that overseers and deacons must manage or lead their own households well (3:4, 5, 12). What does this look like? Why is this important for leaders of God's household (3:15)?

3. The Mystery of Godliness (3:14–16)

First Timothy 3:14–16 summarizes the purpose of the letter and describes the church's identity and mission. How does this understanding of the church serve Paul's aim for instructing and motivating believers toward godly conduct?

The word "mystery" refers to God's secret plan of salvation that he has now gloriously revealed through Jesus Christ (see Rom. 16:25–26; Eph. 3:8–12). What does "the mystery of godliness" mean (1 Tim. 3:16)? How does this relate to the similar phrase "the mystery of faith" in 3:9 and to the remainder of verse 16?

Read through the following three sections on *Gospel Glimpses*, *Whole-Bible Connections*, and *Theological Soundings*. Then take time to consider the *Personal Implications* these sections may have for you.

▶ Gospel Glimpses

A RANSOM FOR ALL. Earlier, Paul declared that "Christ Jesus came into the world to save sinners" (1 Tim. 1:15), and in 2:6 he explains how Jesus secured our salvation by giving "himself as a ransom for all." "Ransom" is the price paid for someone's freedom. Jesus' ransom was an act of *substitution*—the innocent God-man died in our place (Mark 10:45). Jesus did not offer himself as a ransom under coercion or threat; he willingly sacrificed his life to save us, the consummate act of service and love (Eph. 5:2). This ransom was "for all." Some interpreters explain that, while God desires to save all individuals without exception, and Jesus' death potentially atoned for all, he actually saves only believers. More likely, 1 Timothy 2:6 means that Jesus accomplished the salvation of every one of his people from all social classes and ethnic groups (see 2:1 and 4:10). In contrast to the narrow exclusivism promoted by false teachers in Ephesus, Paul stresses that Jesus saves all sorts of people, not just one tribe. This precious truth fuels our prayers and witness to all people, including rulers and Gentiles (2:2, 7).

SAVED THROUGH CHILDBIRTH. God saves undeserving sinners not because of their works but because of his own mercy and grace in Christ Jesus (see 1 Tim. 1:15–16; Titus 2:11; 3:5). Thus, 1 Timothy 2:15 cannot mean that women *merit* salvation or secure God's eternal favor through childbearing. There are three common interpretations of the difficult phrase "saved through childbearing." First, Paul may mean that God will preserve married women who embrace their God-given role of bearing and raising children (compare 5:10). Second, this verse may recall the messianic promise in Genesis 3:15, fulfilled when Jesus of woman" (Gal. 4:4). Third, childbirth was dangerous in the ancient world, and women often prayed for the gods to "save" them physically during childbirth. Thus, 1 Timothy 2:15 may promise safety for Christian women who may want to avoid childbearing due to fear or other reasons. Each interpretation highlights the dignity and importance of women's God-given capacity to bear children and God's saving or preserving work for women as well as men.

THE MYSTERY OF GODLINESS. The "mystery of godliness" (1 Tim. 3:16) explains "the truth" that the church must protect (3:15). The mystery is God's hidden plan now revealed through Christ, which forms the basis for our faith and conduct ("godliness"). Paul explains this mystery with a succinct, poetic summary of Christ's work from both an earthly and a heavenly perspective (v. 16). The first two lines highlight Christ's incarnation and resurrection ("He was manifested in the flesh, vindicated by the Spirit"). The next two lines refer to the proclamation of Christ's work to angels and the nations. The final couplet stresses the acknowledgement of Christ's work, as the nations believed the gospel on earth and Jesus was "taken up" in heavenly glory at his ascension (Acts 1:11). These precious truths are foundational for the church's identity, health, and mission.

Whole-Bible Connections

ONE GOD. "There is one God" (1 Tim. 2:5) summarizes the foundational Old Testament confession: "Hear, O Israel: The LORD our God, the LORD is one" (Deut. 6:4). While the nations worshiped numerous gods, the one true God revealed himself to Israel and called for their total allegiance and love (Deut. 6:5–9). Some Jews in Paul's day, and probably the false teachers in Ephesus, took "our God" in an exclusive sense—he is Israel's God only. In contrast, Paul insists that he must proclaim the good news about the *one* God and *one* mediator, Jesus Christ, to all people, including the Gentiles (1 Tim. 2:7). The Old Testament contains hints that someday all the nations will come to know and worship this true God (Gen. 12:3; Isa. 2:2; Amos 9:12; Zech. 2:11). The one God is Lord of all.

ADAM AND EVE. Paul prohibits women from publicly teaching Scripture or doctrine or exercising authority over men when the church gathers together (1 Tim. 2:12). Paul grounds this instruction in principles derived from Genesis 2–3. First, women should not teach men in the church because of the order of creation: "For Adam was formed first, then Eve" (1 Tim. 2:13, referring to Gen. 2:7, 18). Male headship is rooted in God's creative design, not in tradition or cultural fashions (1 Cor. 11:8–9). Second, "Adam was not deceived, but the woman was deceived and became a transgressor" (1 Tim. 2:14, referring to Gen. 3:13). Elsewhere Paul highlights the disastrous effects of Adam's willful disobedience (Rom. 5:12–18); here and in 2 Corinthians 11:3, he focuses on

Eve's being deceived. The fall inverts the intended order of authority: the man was to obey God and lead the woman, but in Genesis 3 the serpent deceives the woman, and then the man listens to her and disregards God's command. Thus Paul's main point in 1 Timothy 2:12 is that men should reflect God's design by bearing responsibility for teaching and exercising authority over others.

Theological Soundings

A NOBLE TASK. First Timothy 3:1–13 presents the most extensive biblical summary of the qualifications for church leaders. "Overseer" (3:1) is equivalent to "elder" (1 Tim. 5:17; Titus 1:5–7; Acts 20:17, 28) and stresses the leader's essential activity of keeping watch over the church (Heb. 13:17; 1 Pet. 5:2). Paul introduces this passage with another "trustworthy" saying: "If anyone aspires to the office of overseer, he desires a noble task" (1 Tim. 3:1). Godly men who aspire to this office will invest significant time and energy and will face various challenges and stresses, but Paul insists that serving in church leadership is a noble task, a good work. "Above reproach" (3:2) is to be the overarching characteristic of an overseer, and 3:2–7 illustrates what this looks like in one's personal life, family, and dealings with people outside the church. Overseers must demonstrate maturity, integrity, and self-discipline, as well as the ability to teach and care for others.

GOD'S HOUSEHOLD. First Timothy 3:15 offers three important descriptions of the church. First, God's new covenant people are "the household of God." Paul does not mean that the church is a building; rather, it is a family, and God is the authority figure who determines the order and conduct of his household. Second, being "the church of the living God" means that the true God dwells among his redeemed people. Third, Paul describes the church's identity and role using temple imagery. The church is a "pillar" in that it upholds and displays the truth of the gospel for the world to see. The church is built on the foundation of Christ and the apostolic gospel (1 Cor. 3:11; Eph. 2:20), but 1 Timothy 3:15 portrays the church as a "buttress" that protects the truth. Paul writes 1 Timothy to explain how Christians "ought to behave," given their identity as God's household and assembly and their mission of proclaiming and protecting the truth.

Personal Implications

Take time to reflect on the implications of 1 Timothy 2:1–3:16 for your own life today. Consider what you have learned that might lead you to praise God, repent of sin, and trust in his gracious promises. Make notes below on the personal implications for your walk with the Lord of the (1) *Gospel Glimpses*, (2) *Whole-Bible Connections*, (3) *Theological Soundings*, and (4) this passage as a whole.

1. Gospel Glimpses

2. Whole-Bible Connections

3. Theological Soundings

4. 1 Timothy 2:1–3:16

> ### As You Finish This Unit . . .

Take a moment now to ask for the Lord's blessing and help as you continue in this study of 1–2 Timothy and Titus. And take a moment also to look back through this unit of study to reflect on some key things that the Lord may be teaching you.

WEEK 4: INSTRUCTIONS FOR THE CHURCH AND ITS LEADERS

1 Timothy 4:1–6:2a

▲

In the previous section, Paul stressed his purpose in writing and expounded glorious truths about the "mystery of godliness" (1 Tim. 3:14–16). In 4:1–5, Paul warns against the insidious threat of false teaching that undermines the goodness of God's creation. He then offers personal, practical instructions to Timothy, who must persist in faithful teaching and personal piety (4:6–16). Earlier, Paul addressed how men, women, overseers, and deacons should act in the household of God (2:1–3:13). Here Paul offers further instruction to different groups of Christians. Timothy should treat older and younger believers as fathers, brothers, mothers, and sisters in the faith (1 Tim. 5:1–2). Further, the church should honor true widows (5:3–16) and faithful elders (5:17–25), and believing bondservants should honor their masters (6:1–2a).

The Big Picture

First Timothy 4:1–6:2a stresses the vital importance of sound doctrine and godliness for church leaders and various groups of believers.

Reflection and Discussion

Read through the complete passage for this study, 1 Timothy 4:1–6:2a. Then review the questions below concerning this section of 1 Timothy and write your notes on them. (For further background, see the *ESV Study Bible*, pages 2331–2333; available online at esv.org.)

1. False Teaching in Later Times (4:1–5)

First Timothy 4:1 relates a clear prophecy concerning false teaching "in later times." What does Paul mean by "later times"? Do New Testament writers understand "the last days" or "later times" to be still wholly future, or already begun? Consider the context of 4:1–5 and Acts 2:17; 2 Timothy 3:1; Hebrews 1:2; 1 Peter 1:20; and 2 Peter 3:3.

Paul warns against heretical teaching that forbids marriage and requires abstinence from certain foods, and he stresses the goodness of God's creation (1 Tim. 4:1–5). In your own words, restate Paul's argument in verses 4–5. In what sense are food and other created things inherently "good" (see Gen. 1:29, 31; 9:3; Eccles. 9:7–9)? How should believers respond to God's good creation?

2. Teach and Model Sound Doctrine (4:6–16)

Godliness is an important word in 1 Timothy (see 1 Tim. 2:2, 10; 3:16; 4:7–8; 5:4; 6:3, 5–6, 11). What does Paul mean by godliness? Why is it so important, according to 4:8?

First Timothy 4:6–16 stresses the vital importance of sound doctrine and godly living for Christian ministers. In the table below, record commands that relate to these two essential concerns.

Sound Doctrine	Godly Living

How does the profile of a "good servant of Christ Jesus" (1 Tim. 4:6) contrast with Paul's description of false teachers in 1:3–7; 4:1–3; and 6:1–5? Identify at least three differences.

3. Encourage Older and Younger Believers (5:1–2)

Paul exhorts Timothy, "Let no one despise you for your youth" (1 Tim. 4:12), and "Flee youthful passions" (2 Tim. 2:22). What "youthful passions" must Timothy avoid in his dealings with older and younger men and women in the church (1 Tim. 5:1–2)? How does this relate to the requirement that overseers be "above reproach" (3:2)?

4. Honor Widows (5:3–16)

First Timothy 5:3–16 discusses three different groups of widows. Which widows should the church financially support? Why should the church not offer such assistance to younger widows (5:12–15)?

What reasons does Paul offer in 1 Timothy 5:4, 8, 16 to motivate believers to provide for their relatives? How does this relate to the foundational command to "Honor your father and your mother" (Ex. 20:12; compare Mark 7:10; Eph. 6:2)?

5. Honor Elders (5:17–25)

What does it mean for elders who rule well to be "worthy of double honor" (1 Tim. 5:17)? Consider Paul's support for this command in 5:18 and the meaning of "honor" in 5:3.

How should the church handle accusations against elders, according to verse 19? How does this text reflect the principle stated in Deuteronomy 19:15?

6. Honor Masters (6:1–2a)

How does the gospel inform bondservants' identity, motivations, and obligations toward their masters (1 Tim. 6:1–2)? Compare Colossians 3:11, 22–25; Ephesians 6:5–9; and Titus 2:9–10. What principles do these verses offer for Christians in the workplace?

Read through the following three sections on *Gospel Glimpses, Whole-Bible Connections*, and *Theological Soundings*. Then take time to consider the *Personal Implications* these sections may have for you.

Gospel Glimpses

THE SAVIOR OF ALL. Salvation is a major theme in the Pastoral Epistles. First Timothy emphasizes both the universality and the particularity of God's salvation. God is "Savior of all people" (4:10; compare 2:4) and he is also "our Savior" (1 Tim. 1:1; 2:3; compare Ps. 65:5; Isa. 12:2). First Timothy 4:10 brings together the universal and the particular aspects of divine salvation: God is the "Savior of all people, especially of those who believe." The Greek word *malista* ("especially") qualifies or defines a general declaration with a specific statement (1 Tim. 5:8, 17; 2 Tim. 4:13; Titus 1:10). God's saving power and loving concern are not restricted to one tribe or class; rather, anyone from any people may believe the gospel and thus be saved. This truth fuels believers' prayers for "all people" and missionary outreach to the nations, while confronting ethnocentrism in the church (1 Tim. 2:1, 7; 2 Tim. 4:17).

UNSHAKABLE HOPE. Hope is a frequent theme in 1 Timothy. Christians are marked by unshakable confidence in God to fulfill all his promises and to do good to his people forever. Christ Jesus is "our hope" (1:1). Believers do not hope mainly for restored health, freedom from pain, or reunion with loved ones but for Jesus Christ himself, who redeemed us from sin and will return to be with us forever (Titus 2:13–14). Christians' hope in God motivates godliness, which has eternal value (1 Tim. 4:8–10). Paul commends godly widows who pray continually for God to supply their needs (5:5).

Whole-Bible Connections

THE GOODNESS OF CREATION. First Timothy 4:1–5 confronts a dangerous false teaching that restricted marriage and eating certain foods based on a misunderstanding of the law and a warped view of God's creation. Paul's response avoids the two ditches of licentiousness and asceticism, both of which sinfully misconstrue creation's inherent goodness (Gen. 1:31) and its purpose to glorify God and benefit his people. Food was a particularly controversial issue for the early church, because many professing Jews still strictly followed Old Testament dietary laws and viewed Gentiles and their food as "unclean." But Jesus declared all foods clean (Mark 7:19). Christians are distinguished from the world not by their diet or by circumcision but by believing in Christ and loving others through the Spirit's power (Acts 11:17–18; Gal. 5:6). Believers who know the truth should receive foods created by God "with thanksgiving" (1 Tim. 4:3–4).

THE LABORER DESERVES HIS WAGES. Elders who rule well and labor in preaching and teaching are worthy of "double honor" (1 Tim. 5:17), meaning both respect and remuneration. This is consistent with both the Old Testament and Jesus' teaching (5:18). Paul cites Deuteronomy 25:4, which states a principle that animals are entitled to food while working and thus should not be muzzled (compare 1 Cor. 9:9). Jesus similarly affirms, "The laborer deserves his wages" (Luke 10:7). If even animals are entitled to eat while working, the church should certainly provide for the needs of its leaders who work hard in gospel ministry.

Theological Soundings

GODLINESS. Paul exhorts Timothy to "train yourself for godliness" (1 Tim. 4:7). "Godliness" refers to true Christian living that pleases God. It is not mere behavior modification, superficial spirituality, or religious practice. It is not a means to impress people or achieve worldly gain (6:5). Rather, godliness is rooted in the transformative power of the gospel of grace (1 Tim. 3:16; Titus 2:11–12). Jesus saves us from "ungodliness and worldly passions" to be people zealous for good works (Titus 2:12, 14). Godliness is countercultural and strange in this age since it is fueled by hope in the age to come (1 Tim. 4:8). We train for godliness by regularly reminding ourselves of God's promises secured by the gospel, devoting ourselves to sound teaching, and intentionally seeking to live for God's glory by his power.

CARE FOR WIDOWS. The church should "honor" those who are truly widows (1 Tim. 5:3). This means financially supporting and caring for godly, older widows who have no family to support them and so must depend on their spiritual family. God himself provides justice for the widow (Deut. 10:18), and in the Old Testament he repeatedly commands Israel not to mistreat widows and orphans but to provide food and to act justly toward these vulnerable members of society (Ex. 22:22; Deut. 14:29; 27:19). Jesus himself was not too busy to care for a grieving widow (Luke 7:12). The early church regularly distributed food to widows (Acts 6:1), and believers show the genuineness of their faith by their care for widows and orphans (James 1:27).

> ## Personal Implications

Take time to reflect on the implications of 1 Timothy 4:1–6:2a for your own life today. Consider what you have learned that might lead you to praise God, repent of sin, and trust in his gracious promises. Make notes below on the personal implications for your walk with the Lord of the (1) *Gospel Glimpses*, (2) *Whole-Bible Connections*, (3) *Theological Soundings*, and (4) this passage as a whole.

1. Gospel Glimpses

2. Whole-Bible Connections

3. Theological Soundings

4. 1 Timothy 4:1–6:2a

> ## ▶ As You Finish This Unit . . .

Take a moment now to ask for the Lord's blessing and help as you continue in this study of 1–2 Timothy and Titus. And take a moment also to look back through this unit of study to reflect on some key things that the Lord may be teaching you.

WEEK 5: CONTRAST BETWEEN TRUE AND FALSE TEACHING

1 Timothy 6:2b–21

The Place of the Passage

Paul concludes this letter by reminding Timothy to teach sound doctrine and pursue godly living while confronting false teaching and ungodliness. Chapter 6 includes several parallels to chapter 1:

- Paul directs Timothy to teach sound doctrine and pursue love (1 Tim. 1:3, 5; 6:2, 11).
- The opponents lack understanding and have departed from the truth; they teach a "different doctrine" that leads to controversy and vain discussion (1:3–7; 6:3–5).
- Paul corrects misunderstandings concerning the law and godliness (1:7–10; 6:5–6).
- Paul offers praise to God, the immortal, invisible, glorious King (1:17; 6:15–16).
- Paul charges Timothy to guard what is "entrusted" to him (1:18; 6:20).

The exhortation to "teach and urge these things" (6:2b) summarizes Paul's previous instructions to believers in 5:1–6:2a. He then corrects his opponents' false doctrine, morality, motivations, and understanding of wealth before offering a positive alternative for believers who hope in God (6:3–19). The letter closes with an urgent appeal for Timothy to guard the apostolic gospel entrusted to him (6:20).

The Big Picture

In 1 Timothy 6:2b–21, Paul charges Timothy to guard the gospel, teach sound doctrine, and pursue a life of godliness.

Reflection and Discussion

Read through the complete passage for this study, 1 Timothy 6:2b–21. Then review the questions below concerning this section of 1 Timothy and write your notes on them. (For further background, see the *ESV Study Bible*, pages 2333–2334; available online at esv.org.)

1. Negative: False Teachers Motivated by Gain (6:2b–10)

What standards does Paul give for sound teaching in the following verses: 1 Timothy 1:10b–11; 3:16; 4:16; 6:2b–4; Titus 1:1? How does gospel-centered doctrine make a difference in our daily lives?

First Timothy 6:3–5 describes the character and motivations of false teachers. Note at least three contrasts with the profile of qualified overseers in 3:1–7.

What does Paul mean by "contentment" in 1 Timothy 6:6? Compare Philippians 4:11 and Hebrews 13:5. What is the opposite of "godliness with contentment," according to 1 Timothy 6:5, 9? What motivation for contentment does Paul give in 6:7–8?

2. Positive: Godly Teachers Motivated by Eternal Life (6:11–16)

First Timothy 6:11–16 presents a positive alternative to the opponents' greed, ungodliness, and worldliness (6:3–10). What must Timothy "flee" and "pursue," according to 1 Timothy 6:11 and 2 Timothy 2:22? Why is Timothy's personal conduct so important for his ministry as Paul's apostolic delegate? Compare 1 Timothy 4:11–16.

What was Jesus' "good confession" before Pilate (1 Tim. 6:13)? Compare Matthew 27:11 and John 18:33–37. How does Jesus' faithful testimony relate to Timothy's "good confession" (1 Tim. 6:12)? Compare 2 Corinthians 9:13 and Romans 10:9–10.

What does Jesus' "appearing" refer to in 1 Timothy 6:14? Compare 2 Thessalonians 2:8; 2 Timothy 1:10; 4:1, 8; Titus 2:13. How does this "appearing" motivate Timothy to heed Paul's charge in 1 Timothy 6:13–14?

3. Charge to the Wealthy (6:17–19)

What is the "present age" in 1 Timothy 6:17? Compare 2 Timothy 4:10; Titus 2:12; Galatians 1:4. How does our expectation of the future (1 Tim. 6:19) or the coming age (Eph. 1:21) shape our present conduct and priorities?

First Timothy 6:17–19 presents an alternative to the destructive greed and worldliness of those desiring riches (6:9). Paul summons wealthy Christians to hope in God, to "be rich in good works," and to give generously to others. How does this passage illustrate Jesus' famous teaching concerning money and possessions in Matthew 6:19–24?

4. Guard the Gospel (6:20–21)

What is the "deposit" that Timothy must guard (1 Tim. 6:20)? Compare Paul's instructions in 2 Timothy 1:12–14 and 2 Timothy 3:14–15 and his own calling in 1 Timothy 1:11 and 2:7.

Paul opened this letter by addressing Timothy and praying that he would experience grace, mercy, and peace (1:2). First Timothy closes in Paul's customary fashion, with the benediction "Grace be with you" (6:21). In Greek, "you" is plural here and in the closing prayers in 2 Timothy 4:22 and Titus 3:15. Why do you think Paul closes with a corporate benediction? How does this letter address both Timothy and the wider church through him?

Read through the following three sections on *Gospel Glimpses, Whole-Bible Connections*, and *Theological Soundings*. Then take time to consider the *Personal Implications* these sections may have for you.

▶ Gospel Glimpses

THE LORD'S APPEARING. Paul charges Timothy to "keep the commandment unstained and free from reproach until the appearing of our Lord Jesus Christ" (1 Tim. 6:14). *Appearing* refers to Jesus' return, his second coming at the end of the age. At his first coming, Jesus Christ came to rescue sinners as the long-awaited Messiah (1 Tim. 1:15; 2 Tim. 1:10). At his second coming, the Lord Jesus will return in glory "to judge the living and the dead," establish his kingdom, and bring final salvation for his people (2 Tim. 4:1, 8; Titus 2:13). Believers love and long for the Lord's appearing; it is "our blessed hope," the goal of history and of our lives. The hope of Jesus' return encourages believers to endure suffering and also to pursue godliness (1 Tim. 6:14; 2 Tim. 4:6–8). "Our Lord, come!" (1 Cor. 16:22).

GUARD THE DEPOSIT. A deposit is something valuable that an owner entrusts to another for safekeeping. Paul charges Timothy to "guard" the deposit entrusted to him (1 Tim. 6:20; 2 Tim. 1:14). The "deposit" entrusted to Timothy is the gospel message of Jesus Christ. God has "entrusted" the gospel to Paul (1 Tim. 1:11), who instructs Timothy to "entrust" what he has heard from Paul to "faithful men, who will be able to teach others also" (2 Tim. 2:2). Faithful leaders guard the gospel against threats, proclaim and model its life-changing truth and power, and entrust it to others through intentional discipleship and training.

Whole-Bible Connections

LOVE OF MONEY. Money promises security and pleasure, but those who love money will never have enough to be satisfied (Eccles. 5:10). Jesus taught plainly, "You cannot serve God and money," and the Pharisees ridiculed this teaching because they loved money themselves (Luke 16:13–14). Like the Pharisees, Paul's opponents supposed that devout religious practice was a "means of gain" (1 Tim. 6:5). Clamoring after riches brings not satisfaction but sorrows and ultimate "ruin and destruction" (6:9–10). Riches are fleeting and uncertain (6:7, 17), but the solution is not asceticism or vows of poverty. Rather, believers should be content with what they have and should bank their hopes on God, who abundantly provides for his people (6:8, 17). Those with financial means should be generous to others and should "store up treasure" for the life to come (1 Tim. 6:19; Matt. 6:20).

JESUS' GOOD CONFESSION. During Jesus' trial, Pilate asked him, "Are you the King of the Jews?" Jesus responded, "You have said so" (Matt. 27:11). Jesus knew who he was and why he had come to earth (John 18:37–38), so he testified truthfully that he was the messianic King, and he willingly endured unjust suffering and crucifixion. First Timothy 6:12–13 connects Jesus' testimony before Pilate to Timothy's own public affirmation that Jesus is Lord and Messiah. Timothy may have made this "good confession" at his baptism or his commissioning to ministry. Paul reminds his spiritual son of his foundational commitment to follow Jesus in life and ministry (compare 2 Cor. 9:13). Timothy confesses Jesus as Lord and also follows his example of faithful endurance.

Theological Soundings

CONTENTMENT. Ancient Stoic philosophy lauded the moral virtue of contentment or self-sufficiency, regardless of circumstances. Paul stresses that "godliness with contentment is great gain" (1 Tim. 6:6), asserting that "we will be content" with food and clothing (6:8). In support, Paul reasons, "We brought nothing into the world, and we cannot take anything out of the world" (6:7). For Paul, true contentment is not self-sufficiency but rather total dependence on God (Phil. 4:11–13), who richly provides for his people and frees them to live radically generous lives (1 Tim. 6:17–18).

THEOLOGY LEADS TO DOXOLOGY. Theology and doxology are inseparable. Paul moves seamlessly between rigorous theological argument, pastoral exhortation, and joyous exultation in the glory and goodness of God. After expressing his profound gratitude for gospel grace (1 Tim. 1:15–16), Paul gives praise to his King (1:17). In 6:14–16, Paul's meditation on the Lord's appearing leads him again to worship the "blessed and only Sovereign, the King of kings and Lord of lords." Paul celebrates God's sovereign authority, unlimited power, and unique nature. This is sound doctrine that sings!

▶ Personal Implications

Take time to reflect on the implications of 1 Timothy 6:2b–21 for your own life today. Consider what you have learned that might lead you to praise God, repent of sin, and trust in his gracious promises. Make notes below on the personal implications for your walk with the Lord of the (1) *Gospel Glimpses*, (2) *Whole-Bible Connections*, (3) *Theological Soundings*, and (4) this passage as a whole.

1. Gospel Glimpses

2. Whole-Bible Connections

3. Theological Soundings

4. 1 Timothy 6:2b–21

As You Finish This Unit . . .

Take a moment now to ask for the Lord's blessing and help as you continue in this study of 1–2 Timothy and Titus. And take a moment also to look back through this unit of study to reflect on some key things that the Lord may be teaching you.

Week 6: Suffering for Christ

2 Timothy 1:1–2:7

The Place of the Passage

Second Timothy was the apostle Paul's final canonical letter, written from prison to his trusted coworker. Paul writes with confidence in the promises of the gospel, deep affection for his spiritual child, and urgent concern for the church's health and mission.

In 2 Timothy 1:1–5, Paul introduces himself as an apostle, extends God's grace, mercy, and peace to Timothy, and gives thanks to God for Timothy's "sincere faith" (v. 5). "For this reason" (v. 6) links Paul's reasons for gratitude to his pastoral encouragements and exhortations. Timothy must "share in suffering" for the gospel (1:8; 2:3) with Paul and Onesiphorus, who were unashamed of Christ and his people (1:12, 16–18). Timothy must imitate Paul's gospel boldness, follow his "pattern of the sound words" (1:13), and carry on the pattern of biblical discipleship (2:2).

The Big Picture

In 2 Timothy 1:1–2:7, Paul calls Timothy to follow his example of fearlessness in suffering and faithfulness in gospel ministry.

> ### Reflection and Discussion

Read through the complete passage for this study, 2 Timothy 1:1–2:7. Then review the questions below concerning this first section of 2 Timothy and write your notes on them. (For further background, see the *ESV Study Bible*, pages 2338–2339; available online at esv.org.)

1. Paul's Greeting to Timothy (1:1–2)

In 2 Timothy 1:1, Paul introduces himself as an "apostle of Christ Jesus by the will of God according to the promise of the life that is in Christ Jesus." Why do you think Paul begins this way? How do Paul's apostolic calling and his hope in God's promise inform his perspective on present trials? Consider 1:8–12; 2:8–13; 4:6–8.

2. Paul's Gratitude for Timothy's Sincere Faith (1:3–5)

Paul longs to see Timothy again so that he may "be filled with joy" (2 Tim. 1:3–4). Paul frequently mentions believers' joy in the Holy Spirit (Rom. 14:17; Gal. 5:22; 1 Thess. 1:6) and his own joy in fellowship with other Christians (1 Thess. 2:19–20; Phil. 2:2; Philem. 7). What is the relationship between these two sources of joy?

In his prayer of thanksgiving, Paul draws attention to his and Timothy's spiritual heritage (2 Tim. 1:3, 5). What do we know about Timothy's upbringing, according to Acts 16:1 and 2 Timothy 3:15? How might Paul's reference to the faith of Timothy's mother and grandmother encourage Timothy to boldness and endurance (1:6–8)?

Paul recalls Timothy's "sincere faith" (2 Tim. 1:5). What does it mean to have sincere or genuine faith? Consider 1 Timothy 1:2, 5, 19; 4:12; 2 Timothy 1:13; 2:22; 3:10, 15; 4:7.

3. Suffer for the Gospel by God's Power (1:6–11)

Paul reminds Timothy to "fan into flame the gift of God" (1:6). This "gift" may refer to a spiritual gifting for ministry (1 Tim. 4:14), or it may refer to the Holy Spirit, who indwells believers (2 Tim. 1:14). Which interpretation best fits the context? How does 2 Timothy 1:7 explain why Timothy must kindle and not neglect this gift?

Paul urges Timothy, "Do not be ashamed of the testimony about our Lord, nor of me his prisoner" (1:8). How does this command relate to Paul's charge in 1:6–7? Why should Christians be unashamed of Jesus and the gospel? Consider Luke 9:26; Romans 1:16; and 2 Timothy 1:12.

Paul was frequently imprisoned for the gospel (2 Tim. 1:8; 2 Cor. 11:23; Eph. 4:1; Phil. 1:13; Philem. 1:1). Prisons in the ancient world were dark, dirty, and oppressive, and prisoners lacked adequate food and clothing. Even more, friends and family faced pressure to distance themselves from those in prison (2 Tim. 1:15; Heb. 10:34). How should Timothy respond to Paul's chains?

4. Examples of Fearless Faithfulness (1:12–18)

Paul mentions a number of friends in his letters, especially in his closing greetings. He mentions the household of Onesiphorus in 2 Timothy 1:16–18 and 4:19. Why does Paul commend Onesiphorus? How does Onesiphorus illustrate Paul's exhortation to Timothy in 1:8?

5. Entrust the Gospel to Faithful Men (2:1–7)

Timothy must "entrust" the gospel he received from Paul to "faithful men, who will be able to teach others also" (2:2). How does this charge relate to the task of appointing elders or overseers (1 Tim. 3:1–7; Titus 1:5–9; Acts 14:23)? How does Paul's relationship to Timothy offer a model for discipling leaders in the church? See 2 Timothy 1:13; 3:10–11. What is one specific way you can apply this biblical pattern of discipleship in your own life?

In 2 Timothy 1:8, Paul exhorts Timothy to "share in suffering for the gospel by the power of God." In 2:3–6, Paul restates this command and compares Timothy's calling to the soldier, the athlete, and the hardworking farmer. What is the point of these analogies? How do they illustrate important truths of Christian ministry? Compare 1 Timothy 1:18 and 1 Corinthians 9:10, 25.

Read through the following three sections on *Gospel Glimpses, Whole-Bible Connections*, and *Theological Soundings*. Then take time to consider the *Personal Implications* these sections may have for you.

Gospel Glimpses

JESUS OUR LORD. The Greek word *kurios*, translated "Lord," was a title conveying legal authority or ownership. People in Paul's day would have called the emperor "Lord." But *kurios* also regularly translates God's name *Yahweh* in the Greek version of the Old Testament. In Philippians 2:11, Paul declares that every tongue will confess "that Jesus Christ is *Lord*." In other words, Jesus the exalted "Lord" receives the name and worship reserved for God alone (Isa. 45:22–25). One day all people will acknowledge Jesus' deity and supreme authority, but Christians celebrate Jesus as "our Lord" even now (2 Tim. 1:2). This means that we live for his fame, seek to do his will, and trust that he is sovereign and supreme both in the universe and in our own lives.

JESUS ABOLISHED DEATH. Paul reminds Timothy that Jesus Christ "abolished death and brought life and immortality to light through the gospel" (2 Tim. 1:10). This precious truth motivates Paul to proclaim Christ boldly and to endure suffering and possibly execution. Death is the "last enemy" (1 Cor. 15:26), but Christians need not fear death, because our crucified Savior lives, and we will live with him forever.

Whole-Bible Connections

GOD'S INDWELLING PRESENCE. In 1 Timothy 6:20, Paul urged his coworker to "guard the deposit," to steward and safeguard the precious apostolic gospel. He returns to this theme in 2 Timothy 1:14: "By the Holy Spirit who dwells within us, guard the good deposit entrusted to you." Paul's hope for maintaining gospel witness in the world does not rest in Timothy or any human being, however talented or dependable. No, Paul insists that God himself "is able to guard until that Day what has been entrusted to me" (1:12). Further, he reminds Timothy that God's own Spirit dwells in us, as God promised in the Old Testament (Ezek. 36:27). The Spirit's indwelling presence empowers believers for bold gospel witness and guarantees that God's mission will succeed.

Theological Soundings

SPIRITUAL HERITAGE. Paul calls Timothy his "true child in the faith" and "beloved child" (1 Tim. 1:2; 2 Tim. 1:2), but Timothy's first spiritual influence came from believing family members. His father was an unbelieving Gentile, but his believing Jewish mother and grandmother passed on their sincere faith to Timothy (Acts 16:1; 2 Tim. 1:5). Timothy likewise follows Paul's teaching and his faithful way of life (2 Tim. 3:10). Not only that, Timothy "from childhood" has been "acquainted with the sacred writings" (2 Tim. 3:15), another reference to the enduring influence of Lois and Eunice (1:5). Their examples of godliness and faith encourage Timothy to endure suffering and persevere in gospel ministry (2 Tim. 1:6–7; 3:14). These verses show clearly the vital calling of parents and grandparents to teach children the Holy Scriptures and model authentic Christian faith.

DISCIPLESHIP. Discipleship is an integral theme in 2 Timothy. Paul has entrusted the good deposit to Timothy and urges him to entrust this apostolic gospel to others. Biblical discipleship and gospel stewardship involve not only diligently teaching sound doctrine but also living a godly life in Christ Jesus, even if that leads to suffering (3:10–12). Timothy should entrust the gospel to men who are "faithful" (2:2)—dependable and loyal to Christ and his church, unlike the false teachers. Such men should also be "able to teach others," a key characteristic of those qualified to serve as overseers and elders among God's people (1 Tim. 3:2; 5:17; Titus 1:9). Church leaders should view discipleship of future leaders as a significant component of their ministry.

Personal Implications

Take time to reflect on the implications of 2 Timothy 1:1–2:7 for your own life today. Consider what you have learned that might lead you to praise God, repent of sin, and trust in his gracious promises. Make notes below on the personal implications for your walk with the Lord of the (1) *Gospel Glimpses*, (2) *Whole-Bible Connections*, (3) *Theological Soundings*, and (4) this passage as a whole.

1. Gospel Glimpses

2. Whole-Bible Connections

3. Theological Soundings

4. 2 Timothy 1:1–2:7

As You Finish This Unit . . .

Take a moment now to ask for the Lord's blessing and help as you continue in this study of 1–2 Timothy and Titus. And take a moment also to look back through this unit of study to reflect on some key things that the Lord may be teaching you.

WEEK 7: DEALING WITH OPPOSITION IN THE CHURCH

2 Timothy 2:8–3:9

▲

The Place of the Passage

Thus far in 2 Timothy, Paul has called on Timothy to follow his example of teaching and suffering for the gospel. In 2:8–13, Paul urges Timothy to remember Christ and the glorious promises of God. This passage supports Paul's exhortations to Timothy in 2:1–7 and also provides the gospel content of which Timothy must "remind" the church (2:14). In 2:14–3:9, Paul offers instruction for dealing with false teaching. Timothy's opponents quarrel about words and promote ignorant controversies that distract and damage faith (2:14, 16–18, 23). In contrast, Timothy must rightly handle God's Word as a proven worker who faithfully teaches God's people, corrects opponents with gentleness, and models godly character (2:15, 22–25). In 3:1–9, Paul further describes the difficulty and rampant ungodliness that the church faces "in the last days." The opponents are "corrupted in mind and disqualified regarding the faith" (2 Tim. 3:8), and Timothy must avoid such people and remember that they will ultimately fail (3:5, 9).

The Big Picture

In 2 Timothy 2:8–3:9, Paul instructs Timothy to respond to controversy in the church by promoting sound teaching and correcting opponents with gentleness.

Reflection and Discussion

Read through the complete passage for this study, 2 Timothy 2:8–3:9. Then review the questions below concerning this section of 2 Timothy and write your notes on them. (For further background, see the *ESV Study Bible*, pages 2340–2341; available online at esv.org.)

1. Remember Jesus Christ and the Promises of the Gospel (2:8–13)

Jesus called the apostle Paul to a life of suffering and weakness (Acts 9:16; 2 Cor. 12:9–10), and thus Paul suffers "for Christ" and "to advance the gospel" (Phil. 1:12–13). Paul proclaims the gospel of a suffering Savior, and his life illustrates and confirms this message: "I bear on my body the marks of Jesus" (Gal. 6:17). How does Paul explain his suffering in 2 Timothy 1:12; 2:9? What motivates Paul to endure such suffering?

In 2 Timothy 2:9, Paul reminds Timothy that even though he is "bound with chains as a criminal," he is confident that "the word of God is not bound!" Consider Acts 14:19–23; 16:25–34; and Philippians 1:12–14. How do these passages illustrate the important truth that the suffering or imprisonment of Christian leaders may actually be the surprising means of the gospel's advance?

The "trustworthy" saying in 2 Timothy 2:11–13 summarizes believers' glorious hope that they will live and reign with Christ (Rom. 8:17; Rev. 20:4); it warns that

Christ will deny those who deny him (see Matt. 10:32–33); and it reassures us of Christ's faithfulness, which does not change even if we are faithless. How do these verses provide us right perspective and encouragement as we face trials?

2. Faithful Ministers Rightly Handle the Word (2:14–21)

Second Timothy 2:14–18 starkly contrasts faithful ministers like Timothy with false teachers like Hymenaeus and Philetus. Compare each group's motivations, qualifications, and response to the truth.

	Faithful Teachers	False Teachers
Motivations		
Qualifications		
Response to the Truth		

In 2 Timothy 2:20, Paul describes a "great house" that includes some vessels for "honorable" use and others for "dishonorable" use. First Corinthians 12:12–27 uses similar imagery to teach that some Christians who appear to be less honorable or presentable are in fact indispensable for the church body's proper functioning. In 2 Timothy 2:18–21, however, the context suggests that "dishonorable" things are not weaker members of the church but doctrinal error and moral impurity. Why must Timothy "avoid" and "depart from" the dishonorable teaching and practices of false teachers (2:16–19)? What does it mean for Christian leaders to be "useful" to God and "ready for every good work" (2:21)?

3. Faithful Ministers Pursue Righteousness and Avoid Quarrels (2:22–26)

According to 2 Timothy 2:24, "The Lord's servant must not be quarrelsome." This is a qualification of overseers (1 Tim. 3:3) and describes proper conduct for all Christians (Titus 3:2). The Pastoral Epistles frequently link false teachers to church quarrels and controversies (1 Tim. 6:4; 2 Tim. 2:14, 23; 3:9). What are the false teachers quarreling about? Why do they quarrel? What effect does such quarreling have on the church?

How and why should the Lord's servant correct his opponents, according to 2 Timothy 2:24–26? Are Timothy's opponents misguided believers, or are they unbelievers calling themselves Christians? Compare how Paul uses the phrase "knowledge of the truth" in 1 Timothy 2:4; 2 Timothy 3:7; and Titus 1:1.

4. Difficulty in the Last Days (3:1–9)

Does the list of vices in 2 Timothy 3:2–5 describe people inside or outside the church? What does it mean to have the appearance of godliness but to deny its power (3:5)?

Second Timothy 3:2 says that people will be "disobedient to their parents" in the last days. Romans 1:30 includes the same phrase in a list of vices marking those who do not acknowledge God and thus are given over to their sins (1:28). Why is disobedience to parents so serious? Compare Paul's instructions to children

56

in Ephesians 6:1 and Colossians 3:20 and the qualifications for church leaders in 1 Timothy 3:4, 12 and Titus 1:6.

In 2 Timothy 3:8, Paul compares the false teachers to the Egyptian magicians who opposed Moses and Aaron in Exodus 7:19–12, whom later Jewish writings identified as Jannes and Jambres. These magicians imitated some of the miracles performed by Moses and Aaron (Ex. 7:11, 22; 8:7), but they could not replicate the latter plagues and they finally conceded to Pharaoh that God's power was superior to theirs (Ex. 8:18–19). In what ways are Timothy's opponents like these ancient adversaries of Moses and Aaron? How might this comparison encourage Timothy?

Read through the following three sections on *Gospel Glimpses, Whole-Bible Connections*, and *Theological Soundings*. Then take time to consider the *Personal Implications* these sections may have for you.

Gospel Glimpses

THE OFFSPRING OF DAVID. In 2 Samuel 7:12–13, God promised to establish the kingdom of David's offspring forever (compare Ps. 132:11; Isa. 11:1; Jer. 23:5). New Testament writers repeatedly call Jesus "the son of David" (e.g., Matt. 1:1) because he is this long-awaited messianic King. The great King David died, but God raised Jesus from the dead and exalted him to his right hand to validate him as "Lord and Christ" (Acts 2:29–36). Paul proclaimed this good news of King Jesus everywhere he went, and it is the central truth he wants to pass on to Timothy and the church after his death: "Remember Jesus Christ, risen from the dead, the offspring of David, as preached in my gospel" (2 Tim. 2:8).

REPENTANCE. Repentance is more than merely feeling remorse for one's sins. It is a total change of one's mind, heart, and will, turning from sin and Satan toward God. Second Timothy 2:25–26 makes four important points about genuine repentance. First, repentance leads "to a knowledge of the truth"— genuine saving knowledge of God (1 Tim. 2:4). Second, repentance is a gift from God (compare Acts 5:31; 11:18). It cannot be manufactured by human effort, ministry methods, or programs. Third, repentance is linked with coming to one's senses and escaping the Devil's snare. Thus, repentance entails waking up from spiritual stupor and thinking soberly about sin and avoiding it (1 Cor. 15:34). Fourth, believers should hope and pray that their opponents will experience true repentance. In 1 Timothy 1:12–16, Paul recounts that he was once an "insolent opponent" who acted in ignorant unbelief, but he received lavish, undeserved mercy from Jesus Christ.

Whole-Bible Connections

LAST DAYS. The "last days" in Scripture refer to the final period of redemptive history that began with Jesus' first coming and will extend until his return (Acts 2:17; Heb. 1:2). This is a time of increased opposition and ungodliness (2 Pet. 3:3), as well as gospel advance among all nations (Isa. 2:2–5). Paul reminds Timothy, "In the last days there will come times of difficulty" (2 Tim. 3:1), which recalls his similar teaching concerning "later times" in 1 Timothy 4:1. Timothy must be spiritually alert and remember that those who oppose the truth will not ultimately prevail (2 Tim. 3:9).

THE LORD KNOWS HIS PEOPLE. After discussing the damaging effects of false teachers, Paul confidently asserts that "God's firm foundation stands, bearing this seal: 'The Lord knows those who are his,' and, 'Let everyone who names the name of the Lord depart from iniquity'" (2 Tim. 2:19). This verse recalls the Greek translation of Numbers 16:5, where Moses declared, "God knows those who are his," after Korah and 250 well-known men rose up against Moses and Aaron and questioned their leadership over Israel. The next day, Korah and his allies came to the tent of meeting with priestly censers and incense. Moses commanded the congregation, "Depart, please, from the tents of these wicked men" (Num. 16:26). Then the earth opened and swallowed up Korah and his allies, and the Lord's fire consumed the 250 men offering unauthorized incense (Num. 16:31–35). Hymenaeus and Philetus are rebels like Korah and will meet the same fate, for God is a holy judge who will vindicate his chosen people and his truth. Thus, when faced with threats to the gospel and the church's appointed leaders, Paul reminds Timothy that the Lord knows his people and will protect them.

Theological Soundings

GOD'S UNBOUND WORD. In 2 Timothy 2:9, Paul says that he is "bound with chains as a criminal. But the word of God is not bound!" The book of Acts repeatedly illustrates this paradoxical yet profound truth. In Acts 16:23–34, the unjust imprisonment of Paul and Silas leads to gospel witness, and the Philippian jailer and his household are saved. Paul is arrested in Jerusalem in Acts 21 and remains in custody for the rest of the book, but his incarceration provides a providential opportunity to proclaim the gospel before kings and governors and takes him as far as Rome as Christ's ambassador, just as Jesus promised (Luke 21:12; Acts 23:11; 28:30–31). Paul hopes not in his imminent release from prison but in the power of God's Word to overcome all obstacles to save sinners. This hope motivates him to endure suffering and pray for opportunities to speak the Word clearly in every situation (Col. 4:3–4; 2 Tim. 2:10).

DISORDERED LOVE. The vice list in 2 Timothy 3:2–4 includes several references to misplaced or disordered love. Paul says that people will be "lovers of self, lovers of money," and "lovers of pleasure rather than lovers of God." At its root, sin is preferring or loving something created by God more than God himself. It is not sinful for people to desire to be happy or to meet their own needs. Self-love refers to selfishness or narcissism, when self-interest trumps all, when self becomes a god. The love of money is materialism, making money and possessions into a god. Money is useful, but it makes a terrible master, leaving its subjects devastated and empty in the end (1 Tim. 6:9–10, 17–19). "Lovers of pleasure" are hedonists who seek to gratify their physical cravings for sex, food, or the latest buzz at all costs. Such people "serve their own appetites," and "their god is their belly" (Rom. 16:18; Phil. 3:19). God created us to love, enjoy, and admire him forever. No substitute god—self, money, or pleasure—can satisfy our deepest longings.

Personal Implications

Take time to reflect on the implications of 2 Timothy 2:8–3:9 for your own life today. Consider what you have learned that might lead you to praise God, repent of sin, and trust in his gracious promises. Make notes below on the personal implications for your walk with the Lord of the (1) *Gospel Glimpses*, (2) *Whole-Bible Connections*, (3) *Theological Soundings*, and (4) this passage as a whole.

1. Gospel Glimpses

2. Whole-Bible Connections

3. Theological Soundings

4. 2 Timothy 2:8–3:9

As You Finish This Unit . . .

Take a moment now to ask for the Lord's blessing and help as you continue in this study of 1–2 Timothy and Titus. And take a moment also to look back through this unit of study to reflect on some key things that the Lord may be teaching you.

WEEK 8: THE MINISTER'S CONDUCT, COMMITMENT, AND CHARGE

2 Timothy 3:10–4:22

▲

Second Timothy 3:10 begins, "You, however," signaling yet another strong contrast between Timothy and the false teachers and their destructive practices (3:1–9). Paul urges Timothy to persevere in gospel ministry and godly conduct while expecting opposition (3:12). Paul's faithful example (vv. 10–14) and the Scriptures' power (vv. 15–17) should motivate Timothy's perseverance (v. 14). Chapter 4 begins with a solemn charge (v. 1), followed by nine commands related to Timothy's ministry (vv. 2, 5). These commands are motivated by the "time" of dangerous false teaching (vv. 3–4) and Paul's "time" of departure (v. 6). Paul's personal requests in verse 9 ("Do your best to come to me soon") and verse 21 ("Do your best to come before winter") frame the closing section of the letter. Only Luke remains with Paul, and so Paul asks Timothy to visit him soon, bringing along Mark and also Paul's cloak and books (vv. 11–13).

The Big Picture

In 2 Timothy 3:10–4:22, Paul charges Timothy to follow his example of godly conduct, resolute commitment to Christ, and faithful gospel preaching.

Reflection and Discussion

Read through the complete passage for this study, 2 Timothy 3:10–4:22. Then review the questions below concerning this final section of 2 Timothy and write your notes on them. (For further background, see the ESV *Study Bible*, pages 2341–2343; available online at esv.org.)

1. Hold Fast to Scripture and Paul's Example (3:10–17)

Second Timothy 3:10–13 returns again to the important theme of suffering. Why does Paul draw attention to his own suffering here? How do these verses prepare Timothy to respond to the false teachers who oppose the truth in the last days (3:1–9)? How should we respond to suffering and persecution (3:12–14)?

Paul's letters to Timothy and Titus repeatedly emphasize the vital importance of teaching and doctrine that accords with the gospel. What is the model and source for Timothy's teaching, according to 2 Timothy 3:10, 16? How does this prepare Timothy for the warning of 4:3–4?

According to 2 Timothy 3:16–17, God's aim in giving all of Scripture is "that the man of God may be complete, equipped for every good work." Does "the man of God" refer generally to all believers or specifically to Timothy as God's authorized messenger? Compare how this phrase is used in 1 Timothy 6:11 and in the Old Testament (for example, Deut. 33:1; 1 Kings 17:24; 2 Kings 1:9–13). If the phrase does refer to Timothy, how might 2 Timothy 3:16–17 still apply to believers more broadly?

2. Preach the Word (4:1–8)

How do Paul's five exhortations in 2 Timothy 4:2 (preach, be ready, reprove, rebuke, exhort) relate to the "time" in which people will reject sound teaching (4:3–4)? Note the word "for" in verse 3, which typically introduces the reason behind a previous statement. Does the phrase "the time is coming" refer to the distant future, or is it a dramatic description of the serious opposition Paul and Timothy already face? Compare 1 Timothy 4:1–3 and 2 Timothy 3:1.

Paul charges Timothy to "fulfill your ministry" (2 Tim. 4:5; compare Col. 4:17). What does this mean? How does this exhortation relate to the other commands in this verse? Note that Paul uses the same Greek verb translated "fulfill" in 2 Timothy 4:5 to describe his own full proclamation of the gospel among the nations in verse 17.

In 2 Timothy 4:6–8, Paul reflects on the "time" of his own imminent departure. Paul presents his life as a "drink offering," using Old Testament sacrificial imagery (Ex. 25:29). He then reflects further on his imminent death, using three athletic metaphors: (1) a fight or contest, (2) a race, and (3) a victory crown. How does Paul's statement, "I have kept the faith," in verse 7 fit with this imagery? Compare 1 Timothy 6:11; 1 Corinthians 9:24–27. How does Paul's looming death offer support and urgency to Timothy so that he may "be sober-minded, endure suffering, do the work of an evangelist, fulfill your ministry" (2 Tim. 4:5)?

3. Concluding Instructions (4:9–22)

How do Paul's statements about Demas and Mark at the end of this letter (2 Tim. 4:10, 11) illustrate the trustworthy statement in 2:12–13: "If we deny him, he also will deny us; if we are faithless, he remains faithful"? Note that Paul refers to Demas as one of his "fellow workers" in Philemon 24, and Mark (also called John) assisted Paul and Barnabas early in their ministry and then returned home to Jerusalem (Acts 12:12, 25; 13:5, 13).

Acts records Paul's legal hearings before the Jewish council (Acts 22:30–23:10), the governors Felix and Festus (Acts 24:1–25:12), and Agrippa the king (Acts 25:23–26:32). Paul's "first defense" (2 Tim. 4:16) may refer to an initial public hearing before Caesar during his first Roman imprisonment (Acts 27:24; 28:19–20) or to a hearing during a later imprisonment. How does the Lord's presence strengthen Paul to carry out his ministry in difficult circumstances (Acts 18:9–10; 23:11; 27:23–25)? How does 2 Timothy 4:16–17 illustrate the promises of Deuteronomy 31:6, 8?

What does Paul mean in saying that he "was rescued from the lion's mouth" (2 Tim. 4:17)? Compare Psalm 22:13, 21; Daniel 6:22; Hebrews 11:33.

Paul confidently expects the Lord to bring him "safely into his heavenly kingdom" (2 Tim. 4:18). In verse 1 he had reminded Timothy of Jesus' "appearing and his kingdom." In what sense is God's kingdom a present reality for Christians (Rom. 14:17; Col. 1:13)? How will our experience of God's kingdom change when Jesus returns (2 Tim. 4:1, 8, 18; 1 Cor. 15:24, 50)?

Read through the following three sections on *Gospel Glimpses*, *Whole-Bible Connections*, and *Theological Soundings*. Then take time to consider the *Personal Implications* these sections may have for you.

Gospel Glimpses

THE RIGHTEOUS JUDGE. Jesus came first as a suffering Savior (Mark 10:45; 1 Tim. 2:6); he will return as the righteous judge and conquering king (Rev. 19:11–16). It is good news for believers that Jesus will "judge the living and the dead" (2 Tim. 4:1). Jesus will judge with perfect knowledge and fairness—he will right every wrong and give all people what is due them (2 Cor. 5:10; Rev. 22:12). The final judgment serves as a powerful incentive for sinners to repent and believe the gospel (Acts 17:30–31). It also reminds us that the righteous judge took upon himself the judgment we deserved—our debt was cancelled and we are now righteous in Christ (2 Cor. 5:21; Col. 2:14). Thus, believers love and long for Jesus' appearing (2 Tim. 4:8).

GOOD NEWS FOR THE GENTILES. In the Old Testament, God promised to bless "all the nations of the earth" through Abraham's seed (Gen. 22:18). Paul stresses that this promise is fulfilled in Christ (Gal. 3:8, 16). Paul regularly proclaimed Christ to his Jewish kinsmen and longed for their salvation (Rom. 1:16; 10:1), but he was also Jesus' "chosen instrument" to proclaim the gospel among the Gentiles (Acts 9:15; 13:46–47; Gal. 1:16). Paul presents himself as a preacher, apostle, and "teacher of the Gentiles" (1 Tim. 2:7; 2 Tim. 1:11). At the end of his life, he explains that he has fulfilled this calling so that the gospel message would be fully proclaimed among all the nations (2 Tim. 4:17).

Whole-Bible Connections

DRINK OFFERING. In Philippians 2:17 Paul wrote, "Even if I am to be poured out as a drink offering upon the sacrificial offering of your faith, I am glad and rejoice with you all." Now, at the end of his life, this possibility has become a reality: "I am already being poured out as a drink offering" (2 Tim. 4:6). The Old Testament prescribes drink offerings of wine that regularly accompanied grain and animal sacrifices (Ex. 29:40–41; Num. 28:7). Paul describes his impending death or "departure" as a drink offering to God, and the passive voice signals that God is in control and is the one who is pouring out Paul's life. Jesus offered his own life in order to ransom sinners (1 Tim. 2:6), and Paul obediently follows his Lord on the Calvary road, pouring out his life to glorify God, advance the gospel, and strengthen the church (2 Tim. 2:8–10).

RESCUED FROM THE LION'S MOUTH. In 2 Timothy 3:11 and 4:17, Paul recounts how the Lord "rescued" him from his persecutions and sufferings and also "from the lion's mouth"—a vivid biblical metaphor for violent death (Ps. 22:21; Dan. 6:22; Heb. 11:33). Second Timothy 4:16–18 shares several significant parallels with Psalm 22, an important messianic psalm. (1) The psalmist and Paul were both forsaken or deserted (Ps. 22:1; 2 Tim. 4:16). (2) David remembers that God has delivered and rescued his people in the past (Ps. 22:4–5) and prays for deliverance "from the mouth of the lion" (Ps. 22:21). Likewise, God has rescued Paul "from the lion's mouth" and will rescue him in the future (2 Tim. 4:17–18). (3) The psalmist prays for God to come near and strengthen him (Ps. 22:19), and Paul states that "the Lord stood by me and strengthened me" (2 Tim. 4:17). (4) Both David and Paul express confidence that God will establish his kingdom and that all the nations will hear and worship the Lord (Ps. 22:27–28; 2 Tim. 4:17–18). Jesus fulfilled Psalm 22 through his lonely, shameful suffering and his resurrection triumph (Matt. 27:46; John 19:24; Heb. 2:12), while Paul endures present suffering and awaits future resurrection glory. God turned away from Jesus at the cross (Matt. 27:46), but the Lord Jesus stood by Paul in his lonely suffering (2 Tim. 4:17). Further, while Jesus suffered to atone for sin, Paul suffers to make known the gospel among all the Gentiles.

Theological Soundings

GOD-BREATHED SCRIPTURES. Second Timothy 3:14–17 offers one of the fullest biblical explanations of the saving power, divine source, and sufficiency of Scripture. First, the sacred writings have *saving power*: they reveal the true God and proclaim the true gospel, and thus "are able to make you wise for salvation through faith in Christ Jesus" (v. 15). Second, Paul highlights the *divine source* of these writings, which are "breathed out by God" (v. 16) and thus are "sacred," or holy (v. 15). Third, the Holy Scriptures are *sufficient* for life and ministry: they are "profitable for teaching, for reproof, for correction, and for training in righteousness, that the man of God may be complete, equipped for every good work" (vv. 16–17).

PAUL'S SUFFERINGS. Paul reminds Timothy that he has followed Paul's "persecutions and sufferings" (2 Tim. 3:11). He recalls three specific examples of persecutions during his first missionary journey, recounted in Acts 13–14. At Antioch, the Jewish leaders grew jealous of Paul's success, verbally abused him, and stirred up persecution and expelled Paul and Barnabas from the region (Acts 13:45, 50). In Iconium, the missionaries endured similar treatment from the unbelieving Jews and were forced to flee for their lives (Acts 14:1–6). Then, in Lystra, Paul was stoned and left for dead outside the city (Acts 14:19). Paul went to Derbe but later returned to Lystra, Iconium, and Antioch to strengthen the church. He suffered throughout his ministry (Acts 9:16; 20:23), but he references these particular persecutions because they were well known to Timothy, who met Paul in Lystra (Acts 16:1). Paul's gospel boldness and perseverance through severe trials were instrumental in Timothy's coming to faith in Christ and joining Paul in his ministry (Acts 16:3). Timothy must "share in suffering for the gospel" and follow in Paul's steps (2 Tim. 1:8).

Personal Implications

Take time to reflect on the implications of 2 Timothy 3:10–4:22 for your own life today. Consider what you have learned that might lead you to praise God, repent of sin, and trust in his gracious promises. Make notes below on the personal implications for your walk with the Lord of the (1) *Gospel Glimpses*, (2) *Whole-Bible Connections*, (3) *Theological Soundings*, and (4) this passage as a whole.

1. Gospel Glimpses

2. Whole-Bible Connections

3. Theological Soundings

4. 2 Timothy 3:10–4:22

> ### As You Finish This Unit . . .

Take a moment now to ask for the Lord's blessing and help as you continue in this study of 1–2 Timothy and Titus. And take a moment also to look back through this unit of study to reflect on some key things that the Lord may be teaching you.

WEEK 9: APPOINT ELDERS

Titus 1:1–16

▲

The Place of the Passage

Titus does not have a "thanksgiving" section, unlike most of Paul's letters. Instead, as in 1 Timothy, Paul moves immediately from his greeting to the reason for writing. In this short, urgent letter, Paul charges his trusted colleague Titus to bring order to the church in Crete by appointing qualified elders, confronting false teaching, and promoting sound doctrine. The opening chapter comprises three sections: (1) Paul's greeting to Titus (1:1–4); (2) his charge to Titus to establish order and appoint elders (1:5–9); and (3) his challenge to Titus to confront false teachers (1:10–16).

The Big Picture

In Titus 1:1–16, Paul urges his spiritual child Titus to establish order in the church and to appoint elders who are above reproach and committed to sound teaching.

Reflection and Discussion

Read through the complete passage for this study, Titus 1:1–16. Then review the questions below concerning this section of Titus and write your notes on them. (For further background, see the *ESV Study Bible*, pages 2348–2349; available online at esv.org.)

1. Paul's Greeting to Titus (1:1–4)

Titus begins with a lengthy personal introduction of Paul as the letter's sender. How do verses 1–3 present the basis and purpose of Paul's apostleship? Compare Romans 1:1–6. Why do you think Paul emphasizes that he is a "servant of God" and an "apostle of Jesus Christ" in this letter to his close friend Titus?

In Titus 1:1, Paul stresses the vital connection between "knowledge of the truth" and "godliness," which is a summary term for true Christian living that pleases God. Why is godliness an essential hallmark of God's elect people? How do godliness and good works relate to gospel grace, according to Titus 2:11–14 and 3:5, 8?

Why does Paul use the title "our Savior" for both God and Jesus Christ in Titus 1:3–4? Compare 1 Timothy 1:1; 2:3; 2 Timothy 1:10; Titus 1:3–4; 2:10; 3:4–6. How does this divine title prepare us for one of Paul's key emphases in the letter?

2. Titus's Charge: Establish Order, Appoint Elders (1:5–9)

Verse 5 summarizes Titus's ministerial marching orders. Paul left his trusted coworker in Crete to "put what remained into order, and appoint elders in every town." What does this verse suggest about the maturity and condition of the churches on Crete?

Paul refers to "elders," "an overseer," and "God's steward" in Titus 1:5, 7. Are "overseer" and "elders" distinct church offices, or are these terms interchangeable? What does each of these titles emphasize about the responsibilities of church leaders? Look up Acts 20:28; 1 Timothy 5:17; 1 Peter 5:1–3.

Compare the qualifications for elders in Titus 1:6–9 with the list in 1 Timothy 3:1–7. List at least three parallels and three distinct emphases in Titus.

3. Titus's Challenge: False Teachers (1:10–16)

Like Timothy in Ephesus, Titus must confront false teachers in Crete. What does it mean for church leaders to "rebuke" or "silence" false teachers (Titus 1:9, 11, 13; 2:15)? Why is this necessary for the church and for the opponents themselves?

What does Paul say about the false teachers' motives and character in 1:11–13? List at least three contrasts between the false teachers and qualified church leaders in 1:6–9.

The references to the "circumcision party" (v. 10) and "Jewish myths" (v. 14) signal that the false teachers on Crete were promoting a Jewish form of heresy. How does this context help make sense of the contrast between "the pure" and "the defiled" in Titus 1:15? How does this verse reflect Jesus' teaching about ritual and moral purity in Luke 11:38–41?

Read through the following three sections on *Gospel Glimpses, Whole-Bible Connections*, and *Theological Soundings*. Then take time to consider the *Personal Implications* these sections may have for you.

Gospel Glimpses

GOD OUR SAVIOR. Titus 1:3–4 presents both God the Father and Jesus Christ as "our Savior." This divine title prepares readers for one of the great themes of the letter: God's glorious work of salvation. The Old Testament prophets stress that the Lord alone is Savior and Redeemer (Isa. 49:26; 60:16), and the apostle Paul declares that God has now saved his people once for all through the redeeming death of Jesus and the "renewal of the Holy Spirit" (Titus 2:14; 3:4–6). This glorious salvation is the heart of the gospel Paul preaches, and it gives believers peace with God, hope for the future, and motivation for good works (Titus 1:3–4; 2:13–14).

ELECTION. The Bible is clear that God chooses or elects his people for salvation. His sovereign, free choice is determined not by our ethnicity, worthiness, or performance but by his own love and grace (Deut. 7:6–10; Rom. 9:11). The doctrine of election does not weaken the need for preaching and mission but rather enables and motivates gospel ministry. Paul labors as an apostle "for the sake of the faith of God's elect and their knowledge of the truth" (Titus 1:1; compare 2 Tim. 2:10). Paul freely offers the gospel to all, and the elect respond with saving faith when they hear the Word proclaimed (Acts 13:48).

Whole-Bible Connections

GOD'S STEWARD. In Titus 1:7, Paul describes the overseer in the church as "God's steward." A steward is one who manages the household and property of his master (Luke 12:42). Christian leaders must remember that the church is

God's household (1 Tim. 3:15); their job is to oversee, protect, and steward their master's property according to his standards and purposes. To execute this charge faithfully, overseers must "guard the good deposit" of the gospel of Jesus Christ (2 Tim. 1:14), since it is the church's foundation, standard for truth, and fuel for godly living and mission. Titus's opponents are "insubordinate," seeking personal gain and lacking self-control (Titus 1:10–12). In contrast, faithful stewards of God's people must be "above reproach" in all areas of their lives (1:7).

TRUE PURITY. Under the old covenant, Israelites became defiled or unclean by eating unclean food, touching a corpse, contracting certain diseases, or having bodily discharges. Such ritual defilement required atonement or purification in order to be "clean" before God. Jesus later "declared all foods clean" and taught that people are truly defiled not by external things but by sin and evil desires (Mark 7:18–23). Similarly, the Jewish false teachers on Crete who insisted on ritual purity demonstrated by their works that "their minds and their consciences are defiled" (Titus 1:15). True believers have a pure heart, good conscience, and sincere faith; Christians prioritize love, not food laws (1 Tim. 1:5; Rom. 14:20).

Theological Soundings

GOD NEVER LIES. Our world is full of half-truths and spin. But our God is completely truthful; he "never lies" (Titus 1:2). He is not fickle or unfaithful, unlike human beings (Num. 23:19; 2 Tim. 2:13). God promised and has now revealed the way of eternal life for his people through the preaching of the apostles (Titus 1:2–3). Therefore, believers—and especially overseers—should hold firm to God's "trustworthy word" as the foundation of their lives (1:9).

BELIEVING CHILDREN. As stewards of God's church, elders should demonstrate godly management and oversight of their own homes. According to Titus 1:6, their children should be "believers," or "faithful" (ESV footnote). Elders cannot guarantee that their children will come to faith in Christ, but they should teach them the gospel and model lives of godliness for their families. Those of their children who are still living at home should be "submissive" to their authority (1 Tim. 3:4) and act in an appropriate, faithful way. These children should not have a reputation for debauchery or insubordination—sins that characterize false teachers and unbelievers (Titus 1:10, 12). Those who aspire to serve as overseers in the church should demonstrate godly servant leadership in their own homes.

Personal Implications

Take time to reflect on the implications of Titus 1:1–16 for your own life today. Consider what you have learned that might lead you to praise God, repent of sin, and trust in his gracious promises. Make notes below on the personal implications for your walk with the Lord of the (1) *Gospel Glimpses*, (2) *Whole-Bible Connections*, (3) *Theological Soundings*, and (4) this passage as a whole.

1. Gospel Glimpses

2. Whole-Bible Connections

3. Theological Soundings

4. Titus 1:1–16

As You Finish This Unit . . .

Take a moment now to ask for the Lord's blessing and help as you continue in this study of 1–2 Timothy and Titus. And take a moment also to look back through this unit of study to reflect on some key things that the Lord may be teaching you.

Week 10: Teach
Sound Doctrine

Titus 2:1–15

The second chapter of Titus offers a positive vision for the church that contrasts with the opponents' false teaching and immorality in chapter 1 (vv. 10–16). This chapter begins and ends with commands to "teach" or "declare" that which accords with sound doctrine (2:1, 15). In verses 11–14, Paul explains the gospel foundation underpinning the behavior he calls for in verses 2–10. This sound doctrine should produce godly living among various groups in the church: older men (v. 2), older and younger women (vv. 3–5), younger men (v. 6), Titus himself (v. 7–8), and bondservants (vv. 9–10). The grace of God saves sinners; it also instructs and empowers his people to turn from ungodliness and worldly passions to pursue godliness and good works as we wait for Jesus' return (vv. 11–14).

The Big Picture

In Titus 2:1–15, Paul calls Titus to teach sound, gospel-centered doctrine that produces good works among God's people.

> ## Reflection and Discussion

Read through the complete passage for this study, Titus 2:1–15. Then review the questions below concerning this section of Titus and write your notes on them. (For further background, see the *ESV Study Bible*, pages 2349–2350; available online at esv.org.)

1. Good Works for God's People (2:1–10)

Titus 2:1 introduces the overarching theme for the chapter: "But as for you, teach what accords with sound doctrine." "Sound" or "healthy" doctrine/teaching is a key theme in the Pastoral Epistles (see 1 Tim. 1:10; 6:3; 2 Tim. 1:13; 4:3; Titus 1:9; 2:1). What are at least three characteristics of sound doctrine mentioned in these verses? How does this teaching relate to being "sound in faith" (Titus 1:13; 2:2)?

Titus 2:2–10 addresses the intended effects of sound doctrine in the lives of people within the church, beginning with "older men" (v. 2). How do the characteristics of older men reflect the qualifications of overseers and deacons in 1 Timothy 3:1–10 and Titus 1:5–9? How do you see these qualities in the leaders of your church?

Paul calls believers to live in accordance with sound doctrine (Titus 2:2–10). Why do you think Paul repeatedly stresses the need for various groups of Christians to display self-control (2:2, 5, 6) and proper speech (2:3, 8, 9)? How does this relate to the doctrinal and moral problems of the churches in Crete (Titus 1:10–16)?

"Self-control" refers to prudence, self-restraint, and moderation in the face of sin and worldly passions. It is an evidence of gospel transformation (Titus 2:12; Gal. 5:23). What does self-control look like for older and younger men and younger women in this passage? What is one way that you might grow in the area of self-control?

In Titus 2:5, 8, and 10, Paul highlights the goals or aims of believers' godly conduct: "*that* the word of God may not be reviled. . . . *so that* an opponent may be put to shame, having nothing evil to say about us. . . . *so that* in everything they may adorn the doctrine of God our Savior." What do these three purpose statements have in common? How do they relate to the overarching concerns of this letter?

2. The Gospel Foundation for Good Works (2:11–15)

How do verses 11–14 relate to the instructions to various groups in the church in verses 2–10? Note the word "for" in verse 11, which typically indicates a support or explanation for what precedes. How does the gospel of grace empower God's people for good works?

Why does Paul shift from "all people" in verse 11 to "us" in verse 12? How might verses 12–14 clarify the meaning of "salvation for all people"? Compare 1 Timothy 2:4 and 4:10.

How does Titus 2:11–14 summarize our past, present, and future as Christians?

How frequently do you reflect on the sure promise of Jesus' return? How does "our blessed hope" relate to our lives in the present (Titus 2:13–14)?

Titus 2:14 declares that Christ "gave himself for us to redeem us from all lawlessness." The word "redeem" means to liberate or rescue from oppression. Consider the following Old Testament references to redemption: Exodus 6:6; 15:13; Deuteronomy 9:26; Psalm 130:8; Isaiah 43:1; 44:22; Micah 6:4. What does God redeem his people from? What is the effect or goal of redemption, according to Titus 2:14?

Read through the following three sections on *Gospel Glimpses, Whole-Bible Connections*, and *Theological Soundings*. Then take time to consider the *Personal Implications* these sections may have for you.

▶ Gospel Glimpses

THE GRACE OF GOD. God's grace is his extravagant, generous favor freely given to undeserving people who could never pay him back. In Titus 2:11, Paul explains that "the grace of God has appeared, bringing salvation for all people." In Exodus 34:6, the Lord revealed himself to Moses as a "God merciful and gracious," yet God's grace has "appeared" in the fullest way in the revelation of "our great God and Savior Jesus Christ" (Titus 2:13), who is "full of grace and truth" (John 1:14). This grace transformed Paul's own life when he was a blasphemous opponent of the Messiah Jesus (1 Tim. 1:12–14), and his great ambition is to testify to the good news of this grace (Acts 20:24).

GOSPEL EDUCATION. Titus 2:12 describes the ongoing effect of gospel grace as "training" (Greek *paideuō*). Elsewhere Paul uses this word for correction or discipline (1 Tim. 1:20; 2 Tim. 2:25). Here and in 2 Timothy 3:16, *paideuō* refers to training or instruction in godliness and righteousness. Greek education aimed to civilize students and train them in virtue, but the Cretans fell far short of these cultural standards (Titus 1:12). Gospel grace saves us from the punishment our sins deserve, but it does not stop there. Grace is also our master teacher, training and transforming us to live as God's holy people, according to God's own standards and for his purposes.

Whole-Bible Connections

THE PRESENT AGE. The Bible frequently distinguishes between "this age" and the "age to come" (see Matt. 12:32; Eph. 1:21). The present age follows worldly wisdom, values, and rulers that are doomed to pass away (1 Cor. 2:6). Christians have been delivered from the "present evil age" (Gal. 1:4)—we have received the end-time gift of the Holy Spirit and new birth to a living hope (Acts 2:17; 1 Pet. 1:3)—but we still wait for the full experience of eternal life in the age to come (Luke 18:30). Christians should not set their hopes on the riches, pleasures, and accolades of this age (1 Tim. 6:17; 2 Tim. 4:10). Rather, the grace of God trains believers for self-control, righteousness, and godliness in this age while they eagerly wait for the return of Jesus Christ the Savior (Titus 2:12–13).

A PEOPLE FOR HIS OWN POSSESSION. In the Old Testament, God rescued Israel from Egypt and chose them to obey his voice, keep his covenant, and be his "treasured possession among all peoples" (Ex. 19:5; compare Deut. 7:6; Ps. 135:4). Israel broke the covenant, defiled themselves with idolatry and immorality, and received God's just judgment. However, God promised that one day he would cleanse them from their sins, put his Spirit within them to empower obedience, and restore them to their status as his people (Ezek. 36:25–28). This is precisely what God has accomplished through Jesus Christ, who redeems and purifies us, the church, to be "a people for his own possession who are zealous for good works" (Titus 2:14). We have been bought with Christ's precious blood, and we belong to God forever.

Theological Soundings

SUBMISSION. The short book of Titus repeatedly stresses the importance of biblical submission to authority. The opponents in Crete are "insubordinate," meaning they are rebellious and unwilling to submit to God and his standards (Titus 1:10). Children should honor and obey their parents (Eph. 6:1–2); if a man's children are insubordinate and openly rebellious, he is unqualified to serve in church leadership (Titus 1:6). Positively, older women should encourage younger wives to love and submit to their husbands, and "bondservants are to be submissive to their own masters in everything" (2:5, 9). Believers should also "be submissive to rulers and authorities" (3:1). These verses are not a blank check for husbands, fathers, masters, or governing authorities to exercise their authority in a harsh or abusive way, for everyone is subject to Christ's supreme authority and must answer to him (2 Cor. 5:10). Paul calls not simply for lip service or outward respect for authority but for a heart attitude of faith in God, love, kindness, and self-control. Christians submit to authority "as to the Lord and not to man" (Eph. 6:7), and they do so in order that "the word of God may not be reviled" (Titus 2:5).

WINE. Paul stresses that "everything created by God is good" (1 Tim. 4:4) and calls Christians to eat and drink and do everything to God's glory (1 Cor. 10:31). Paul rejects legalistic restrictions on food and drink because they promote self-made religion rather than true godliness (Col. 2:16–23; 1 Tim. 4:3). Paul also repeatedly warns Christians against drunkenness, gluttony, and self-indulgence (1 Tim. 3:3, 6; 5:6; Titus 1:6, 12; 2:3). These sins characterize people who are enslaved to their appetites and are living without hope (1 Cor. 15:32; Phil 3:19). The gospel of grace saves Christians from enslavement to worldly passions that cannot satisfy our souls (Titus 2:11; 3:3), and it trains and empowers us to live with self-control and godliness (2:12). Believers—especially church leaders—should model self-control, moderation, prudence, and thankfulness to God in eating and drinking and in all things.

Personal Implications

Take time to reflect on the implications of Titus 2:1–15 for your own life today. Consider what you have learned that might lead you to praise God, repent of sin, and trust in his gracious promises. Make notes below on the personal implications for your walk with the Lord of the (1) *Gospel Glimpses*, (2) *Whole-Bible Connections*, (3) *Theological Soundings*, and (4) this passage as a whole.

1. Gospel Glimpses

2. Whole-Bible Connections

3. Theological Soundings

4. Titus 2:1–15

As You Finish This Unit . . .

Take a moment now to ask for the Lord's blessing and help as you continue in this study of 1–2 Timothy and Titus. And take a moment also to look back through this unit of study to reflect on some key things that the Lord may be teaching you.

WEEK 11: SAVED FOR GOOD

Titus 3:1–15

▲

The Place of the Passage

The apostle Paul concludes his short letter to his coworker Titus by stressing the priority of good works (Titus 3:1–2, 8, 14), the power of the gospel of grace (vv. 3–7), and the need to avoid quarreling and division (vv. 2, 9–11). In verses 12–15, Paul offers final instructions and greetings to Titus and the believers with him on Crete. The gospel is central to this chapter, as it is to the whole letter. Because of God's saving work in Christ, believers experience cleansing from sin, new birth, justification, adoption as heirs of eternal life, and spiritual empowerment for good works.

The Big Picture

In Titus 3:1–15, Paul explains that God saves his people *from* sin and *for* good works.

▶ Reflection and Discussion

Read through the complete passage for this study, Titus 3:1–15. Then review the questions below concerning this section of Titus and write your notes on them. (For further background, see the *ESV Study Bible*, pages 2350–2351; available online at esv.org.)

1. Good Works toward Outsiders (3:1–2)

Titus 2:1–10 addressed how sound doctrine should produce godliness and good works among various groups of people within the church. Now, in 3:1–2, Paul instructs Titus to remind believers how they should act toward governmental authorities and "all people." What does it mean to "be submissive to rulers and authorities" (v. 1)? Compare Romans 13:1 and 1 Peter 2:13. How does this relate to Paul's exhortation, in 1 Timothy 2:1–2, to pray for those in authority?

2. The Gospel Foundation for Good Works (3:3–8)

In Titus 3:3–7, Paul magnificently recounts what we once were, *apart* from Christ and what God did to save us *through* Christ. These verses provide a gospel basis for the instructions in verses 1–2 (note the word "for" in v. 3). Why is it important for Paul at this point in the letter to remind Christians that they were once foolish, disobedient, led astray, enslaved by sin, envious, and hateful? List at least four contrasts between the attitude and actions called for in verses 1–2 and believers' lives before being saved by Christ, described in verse 3.

Titus 3:5 explains that God saved us "by the washing of regeneration and renewal of the Holy Spirit." How does this description of salvation recall the promise of the new covenant in Ezekiel 36:25–27? How does Jesus explain these truths to Nicodemus in John 3:5?

God not only saves us from sin, slavery, and foolishness; he also makes us "heirs according to the hope of eternal life" (Titus 3:7). How does this glorious future inheritance relate to our new identity in Christ? Consider Romans 8:17; Galatians 3:29; 4:7.

Good works are a major theme in Titus. If Christians are saved not because of their works but because of God's mercy (Titus 3:5), why does Paul repeatedly call believers to devote themselves to good works (2:7, 14; 3:8, 14)? How do good works relate to our mission and calling in the world (3:1)? How do good works give evidence of whether our faith in Christ and knowledge of God are genuine (1:16)?

3. Avoid Controversies and Division (3:9–11)

Paul contrasts his teaching concerning what is "excellent and profitable" (v. 8) with the foolish controversies of the false teachers, which are "unprofitable and worthless" (v. 9). What is the biblical standard for what is valuable or beneficial?

Compare 1 Timothy 4:8; 2 Timothy 3:16; and Philippians 4:8. How does this compare with our culture's values today?

_____

_____

_____

_____

_____

In Titus 3:9–11, Paul warns against foolish controversies and divisive people. Note at least three parallels between this passage and Paul's description of our former lives apart from Christ in verse 3. Why should believers avoid, warn, and shun people *in* the church who reflect such behaviors, while showing gentleness and perfect courtesy to those *outside* the church (v. 2)?

_____

_____

_____

_____

_____

Titus 3:10 sets forth a three-step process for correcting and disciplining one who "stirs up division." Why does Paul call for church discipline in response to an unrepentant, divisive person in the church? See 1 Timothy 6:4; 2 Timothy 2:23; Titus 1:10–14. How does Titus 3:11 support the command to "have nothing more to do" with such a person? Compare Paul's instructions here with Jesus' teaching in Matthew 18:15–17.

_____

_____

_____

_____

_____

4. Concluding Instructions (3:12–15)

In his letters, Paul frequently refers to other believers who are vital participants in his missionary work. He writes letters to Timothy and Titus, who are engaged in ministry in Ephesus and Crete, and names several current and former coworkers in 2 Timothy 4:9–21 and Titus 3:12–13, including Tychicus and Apollos. Acts 18:24–19:1 introduces Apollos and describes his ministry in Ephesus and Corinth, while Tychicus is mentioned in Acts 20:4; Ephesians 6:21; Colossians 4:7; and 2 Timothy 4:12. What stands out to you about these two coworkers of the apostle Paul?

Paul plans to send Artemas or Tychicus to Crete so that Titus can leave to visit Paul (Titus 3:12). How does Paul instruct Titus to send Zenas and Apollos on their way in verse 13? Compare similar instructions to send or help Christian workers on their way in Romans 15:24; 1 Corinthians 16:6, 11; and 3 John 6. What are one or two specific ways that Titus 3:13 informs how Christians today should send missionaries?

Read through the following three sections on *Gospel Glimpses, Whole-Bible Connections*, and *Theological Soundings*. Then take time to consider the *Personal Implications* these sections may have for you.

Gospel Glimpses

RENEWAL OF THE HOLY SPIRIT. According to Titus 3:5, salvation includes both "washing" and "renewal." Similarly, Jesus tells Nicodemus, "Unless one is born of water and the Spirit, he cannot enter the kingdom of God" (John 3:5). Both of these passages reflect the hope of the new covenant. In Ezekiel 36:25–27, God promised to cleanse his people from uncleanness and idolatry, replace their hearts of stone with new hearts of flesh, and put his Spirit within them to cause them to obey him. God has provided his people cleansing from sin and defilement through the blood of Christ, and he poured out his Spirit to give them new life, a new power to live to please him, and a new hope of an eternal inheritance (Titus 3:5–7).

JUSTIFIED AND ADOPTED. The Bible declares that every person will appear before God's judgment seat, and the verdict we should all receive based on our works is "guilty." However, Jesus Christ died as a substitute in our place, and his righteousness is imputed to believers as a free gift of grace (Rom. 5:17). God "justifies the ungodly" (Rom. 4:5); he declares guilty people innocent and righteous in his sight because of his righteous Son, Jesus. Titus 3:7 moves from justification to adoption, from the law court to the family, as it describes how believers are adopted into God's family and offered a glorious, undeserved status as "heirs" of eternal life (cf. Rom. 8:16–17).

Whole-Bible Connections

CHURCH DISCIPLINE. Titus 3:10 calls for the church and its leaders to remove a divisive person from church membership if he refuses to respond to multiple warnings. In Matthew 18:15–17, Jesus outlines a similar process for handling sin within the church. Church discipline protects the faith and purity of other believers, guards the truth of the gospel, and promotes the church's holiness and witness in the world. Church discipline is not vindictive or mean-spirited but courageous and loving (1 Tim. 1:5; Titus 1:9). Its goal is repentance and restoration, so that redeemed sinners may become "sound in the faith" (Titus 1:13; compare 1 Cor. 5:5).

ROOT AND FRUIT. In Titus 3:5, Paul stresses that believers are not saved "because of works done by us in righteousness," yet he insists in verse 8 that believers must "devote themselves to good works" (see also 2:7, 14; 3:14). In other words, the "root," or basis, of our salvation and justification is God's mercy, not any works or effort on our part. But at the same time, good works are visible "fruit," or evidence, that Christians have been justified by God's grace and renewed by the Spirit. The false teachers in Crete completely missed this distinction. These opponents insisted on keeping human commandments and the law (Titus 1:14; 3:9), yet their ungodly works demonstrated that they did not truly know the God they taught about (1:16). As Jesus instructed, his followers should recognize false prophets "by their fruits" (Matt. 7:16).

Theological Soundings

WHAT WE ONCE WERE. In Titus 3:3, Paul reminds believers that we were once foolish, disobedient, deceived, and enslaved to passions and pleasures, living lives of malice, envy, and hatred. Believers have no reason to boast. We do not deserve God's favor, and we certainly could not save ourselves through personal improvement, education, or moral reform. Our only hope is the "goodness and loving kindness of God our Savior," who saved us because of his mercy, not because of our righteous deeds (vv. 4–5). Paul reminds Christians of their sinful past so that they will respond rightly to unbelievers inside and outside the church. Believers must see the opponents of Christ as they really are—foolish, disobedient unbelievers who do not truly know God—so that they are not led astray by their false teaching (1:10–14). Christians should also "be ready for every good work" in their dealings in the world for the sake of gospel witness (3:1).

PAUL'S COWORKERS. The apostle Paul was not a "lone ranger"; he regularly traveled and ministered with other believers. The apostolic delegates Timothy and Titus are well known, but Paul refers to four other coworkers in Titus 3:12–13 as well. Artemas and Zenas the lawyer are mentioned only here in the New Testament. The name Artemas probably means "gift of Artemis," a popular deity worshiped throughout the ancient world and especially in Ephesus (see Acts 19:27–28). Artemas heard the gospel—likely through Paul's ministry—and devoted his life to serving not Artemis but Jesus Christ. Tychicus was a Christian from Asia Minor who accompanied Paul on his third missionary journey (Acts 20:4). Paul describes him as a beloved brother, faithful minister, and fellow servant in the Lord, and he sends him to minister in Colossae and Ephesus on his behalf (Col. 4:7–9; Eph. 6:21–22; 2 Tim. 4:12). Apollos, a native of Alexandria, was an eloquent, powerful preacher in Ephesus and Corinth (Acts 18:24–19:1; 1 Cor. 1:12). Paul considered these Christians essential partners in the work of the gospel.

> ### Personal Implications

Take time to reflect on the implications of Titus 3:1–15 for your own life today. Consider what you have learned that might lead you to praise God, repent of sin, and trust in his gracious promises. Make notes below on the personal implications for your walk with the Lord of the (1) *Gospel Glimpses*, (2) *Whole-Bible Connections*, (3) *Theological Soundings*, and (4) this passage as a whole.

1. Gospel Glimpses

2. Whole-Bible Connections

3. Theological Soundings

4. Titus 3:1–15

As You Finish This Unit . . .

Take a moment now to ask for the Lord's blessing and help as you continue in this study of 1–2 Timothy and Titus. And take a moment also to look back through this unit of study to reflect on some key things that the Lord may be teaching you.

WEEK 12: SUMMARY AND CONCLUSION

▲

We conclude our study of 1–2 Timothy and Titus by summarizing the big picture of God's message through these biblical letters. Then we will consider several questions in order to reflect on various Gospel Glimpses, Whole-Bible Connections, and Theological Soundings throughout this portion of the New Testament.

The Big Picture of 1–2 Timothy and Titus

In 1–2 Timothy and Titus, Paul instructs, warns, and encourages his trusted coworkers. Above all, these letters stress two essential priorities of the church: the gospel and discipleship. God has entrusted Paul with the true gospel and appointed him to teach and herald that truth as an apostle (1 Tim. 1:1; 1:11; 2:7). Paul calls Timothy and Titus to guard the good deposit, remain faithful to sound doctrine, and continue in what they have learned from him (1 Tim. 6:20; 2 Tim. 3:14). They should also follow Paul's example and entrust the apostolic gospel to "faithful men who will be able to teach others also" (2 Tim. 2:2). Entrusting the gospel to others involves training and appointing godly overseers in the churches to serve as God's stewards. These stewards must hold firmly to the trustworthy Word, care for God's people, and rebuke false teachers (Titus 1:5–9). The ongoing health of the church and its witness to Christ in the world depends on godly leaders modeling gospel truth and entrusting it to others, who will in turn continue this pattern of discipleship.

These biblical letters celebrate the gospel of grace and warn the church not to accept counterfeit doctrines. The gospel of Jesus Christ is the standard for sound doctrine and the catalyst for good works (1 Tim. 6:3; Titus 2:14). Timothy, Titus, and approved overseers in the church should teach and urge that which promotes godliness, while rebuking false teachers who distort and distract from the truth and deceive and damage the church (Titus 1:9–16). Believers—especially faithful church leaders—will face threats and times of difficulty in the last days, but they must share in suffering for the gospel while remaining confident that "God's firm foundation stands" (2 Tim. 1:8; 2:19; 3:1).

▶ Gospel Glimpses

First and Second Timothy and Titus offer some of the most extensive summaries of the gospel in all of Scripture. The Son of God took on flesh to become the one mediator between God and people and to give his life as a ransom (1 Tim. 2:5–6). Jesus Christ came to rescue, redeem, and purify sinners from lawlessness and for his good purposes (1 Tim. 1:15; Titus 2:14). He has risen from the dead and will return to consummate his saving work (2 Tim. 2:8–12). Paul testifies that his own life is "Exhibit A" for the gospel truth that Jesus Christ saves undeserving sinners because of his extravagant mercy (1 Tim. 1:13–16). Further, this message is truly good news for all people, and Paul's ambition is to teach and herald the saving mercy of Jesus Christ among the nations (1 Tim. 2:7; 2 Tim. 4:17).

Paul is crystal clear that human beings do not deserve salvation in any way. God saves us solely because of his lavish mercy, grace, and electing love, not because of any righteous deeds we perform. We are saved *by* grace, *for* good works: our great God and Savior Jesus Christ "gave himself for us to redeem us from all lawlessness and to purify for himself a people for his own possession who are zealous for good works" (Titus 2:13–14). God's people are marked by godliness and good works, which demonstrate that God has indeed delivered us from the penalty and power of sin and made us alive by his Spirit (Titus 3:3–6).

How have Paul's letters to Timothy and Titus clarified or deepened your understanding of the gospel?

What are a few particular passages in 1–2 Timothy and Titus that have led you to a fresh understanding and grasp of God's grace to us through Jesus?

Reflect on Paul's own testimony of God's saving mercy in Christ in 1 Timothy 1:12–17. How does this passage inform how you might share with others your personal experience of God's extravagant grace?

> ## Whole-Bible Connections

First and Second Timothy and Titus are rich in whole-Bible themes. *God* is the omnipotent, immortal, all-wise Creator and King of all; he is also our Savior (1 Tim. 1:1, 17; compare Isa. 49:26; 60:16). *Jesus Christ* is God's Son, the long-awaited Messiah who came to ransom sinners (1 Tim. 2:5–6; 2 Tim. 2:8; compare 2 Sam. 7:12–16). The *Holy Spirit* has cleansed God's people from sin as he has poured out the Spirit upon them (Titus 3:5), fulfilling the new covenant promises in Ezekiel 36:25–27. *The church* is God's household and his special possession (Titus 2:14; compare Ex. 19:5). *God's enemies* will not prevail because "the Lord knows those who are his." God vindicated Moses in Pharaoh's court and during Korah's rebellion, and he will similarly vindicate faithful leaders in the church while judging false teachers (2 Tim. 2:19; 3:8–9). Additionally, *the Scriptures* provide practical guidance for God's people on matters such as understanding the Law's proper use, celebrating the goodness of creation, caring for widows, honoring church leaders, and handling complaints and accusations (1 Tim. 1:8–11; 4:4; 5:3, 17–19). Paul affirms that the sacred Scriptures are breathed out by God, profitable for his people, and able to make us wise unto salvation (2 Tim. 3:15–16).

How has this study of 1–2 Timothy and Titus filled out your understanding of the biblical storyline of redemption?

How have these letters expanded your understanding of the salvation that Jesus provides?

What connections between 1–2 Timothy and Titus and the Old Testament were new to you?

Theological Soundings

Our understanding of Christian theology is greatly enriched through 1–2 Timothy and Titus. These letters develop, clarify, and reinforce many doctrines and theological themes, including the truthfulness and power of Scripture (2 Tim. 3:16), the difficulty to be expected in the last days (1 Tim. 4:1; 2 Tim. 3:1), the church's identity and mission in the world (1 Tim. 3:15), the priority of discipleship (2 Tim. 2:2), and the qualifications for church leaders (1 Tim. 3:1–13; Titus 1:5–9). Reflect on the key Theological Soundings we have seen throughout Paul's letters to Timothy and Titus.

Has your theology been refined at all during the course of studying Paul's letters to Timothy and Titus? How so?

1. FROM THE SAME STATE AS YOU (BONUS IF SAME CITY TOO)

2. IS BORN IN THE SAME MONTH AS YOU (BONUS IF THE SAME AGE AND SAME BIRTHDAY)

3. LIKES HER COFFEE THE SAME WAY YOU DO

Amy Watson

4. HAS THE SAME FAVORITE DESSERT

How has your understanding of the nature and character of God been deepened throughout this study? Consider especially Titus 3:4–6.

What unique contributions do 1–2 Timothy and Titus make toward our understanding of who Jesus is and what he accomplished through his life, death, and resurrection? Consider especially 1 Timothy 2:5–6 and 2 Timothy 2:8–10.

What specifically do these letters teach us about the human condition and the message of salvation? Consider especially 1 Timothy 1:12–16; Titus 2:11–14; 3:3–7.

Personal Implications

Paul explains that the Word of God is "profitable for teaching, for reproof, for correction, and for training in righteousness" (2 Tim. 3:16). How has your study of 1–2 Timothy and Titus encouraged, challenged, or equipped you?

Paul closes his letter to Titus with this exhortation: "Let our people learn to devote themselves to good works, so as to help cases of urgent need, and not be unfruitful" (3:14). How has this study promoted good works and gospel fruitfulness in your life?

What are two or three specific truths from 1–2 Timothy and Titus that have led you to praise God, turn away from sin, or trust more firmly in his promises?

As You Finish Studying 1–2 Timothy and Titus . . .

We rejoice with you as you finish studying Paul's letters to Timothy and Titus! May this study become part of your Christian walk of faith, day by day and week by week throughout all your life. Now we would greatly encourage you to study the Word of God in an ongoing way. To help you as you continue your study of the Bible, we would encourage you to consider other books in the *Knowing the Bible* series, and to visit www.knowingthebibleseries.org.

Lastly, take a moment to look back through this study. Review the notes that you have written, and the things that you have highlighted or underlined. Reflect again on the key themes that the Lord has been teaching you about himself and about his Word. May these things become a treasure for you throughout your life—this we pray in the name of the Father, and the Son, and the Holy Spirit. Amen.